The Stairway of Surprise

The Stairway of Surprise

Six Steps to a Creative Life

by

Michael Lipson, Ph.D.

ANTHROPOSOPHIC PRESS

Published by Anthroposophic Press
Post Office Box 749
Great Barrington, MA 01230

Library of Congress Cataloging-in-Publication Data

Lipson, Michael, 1957–
    The stairway of surprise : six steps to a creative life /by Michael Lipson.
    p. cm.
    ISBN 0-88010-507-0
    1. Anthroposophy I. Title.
    BP595 .L56 2002
    299'.935—dc21   2002002254

Book design by Studio 31
www.studio31.com

Printed in the United States of America

CONTENTS

Introduction   9

I. Thinking   25

II. Doing   43

III. Feeling   57

IV. Loving   75

V. Opening   89

VI. Thanking   105

Notes   123

I shall mount to paradise by the stairway of surprise.

—Ralph Waldo Emerson

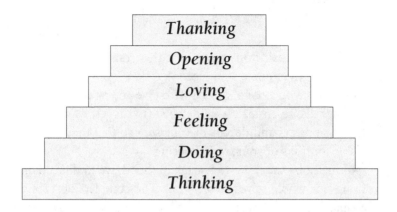

Introduction

There is something *extra* about the human soul. We have more than enough in us, and perhaps too much. Where the granite, the grass, and the seagull keep more or less to their accustomed paths of being, humans are capable of endless creativity (and endless distortion). We are the least predictable thing in creation. Our very essence is surprise.

Human languages and cultures contain vast reaches of what might be called "useless" material: the arts, religion, fiction, invention, play. They go beyond what we need to persist biologically. We are freer from the demands of usefulness than all our friends on the planet. Our inner lives, too, overflow with extras, though some are news and some are old hat: forgiveness, resentment, devotion, nostalgia, invention. I remember asking myself, as a six-year-old child staring out the rear window of our Ford station wagon, "What shall I think about?" I had seen, as children often do in their slow fall from grace, that this something extra, this superfluity in the human soul, needs a task.

It is not the purpose of this book to give you a task, or even to help you find one. Instead the aim here is to suggest ways you can gather the powers and depths of your soul so that they are truly available for tasks of your own choosing.

Normally, by the time we reach adulthood, we find it difficult to bring our whole selves to any task. The complete absorption that small children demonstrate in play and in learning language gives way in later childhood and adulthood to a mind full of distractions, associations, and worries. Yet our powers of absorption never quite disappear. We can always pay *some* attention. This most fundamental human capacity — the capacity to attend — is the human *extra*. It can be strengthened so that we apply ourselves more creatively to our chosen work and play, regaining something of the small child's absolute immersion.

Western tradition has often pointed to the need to strengthen the faculty of attention. In the *Phaedo*, Plato hints in this direction when he has Socrates talk about "gathering" the forces of the soul through philosophy.[1] This book will discuss six aspects of attention, with exercises to strengthen, to "gather," each of them. Formerly, they were known as *concentration of thought, initiative of will, equanimity, positivity, freedom from prejudice,* and *forgiveness.*[2] I have given new names to these six and have adapted them for our day. They are *thinking, doing, feeling, loving, opening,* and *thanking.*

That's a lot of *ings*. I use verbal nouns like "thinking" instead of noun phrases like "concentration of thought" to emphasize the fluid process of the attention. Like music, these six categories are not permanent possessions or things. They exist only in performance, in the moment of carrying them out. A recent book by Rabbi David Cooper proclaims that "God is a verb."[3] Well, these human categories are also verblike and alive.

As with the performance of a musical instrument, these powers of the soul require practice if they are to become significant, and this book suggests how to practice them. Please think of what you read here more as a musical score than as a collection of information. The exercises described will only mean something to you if you actually practice them, in the same way that a musical score only reveals itself when your performance turns it into sound. As the player's skill increases, the music reveals more. It is up to you not simply to receive, but to invent such exercises for yourself — and each time anew.

In a sense, the six powers, and the exercises that promote them, simply represent intensifications of inner functions that we all know we need to develop. We all could benefit from *thinking* with less distraction, more concentration, more invention. We all have difficulty in carrying out our intentions (*doing*). We all could benefit from turning our self-oriented emotions outward, and understanding the world through *feeling*. If we are honest, we admit that we can become more *loving*, and so throw the weight of our awareness on the side of the Good. Through *opening*, or freedom from prejudice, we could find ourselves more available to the intuitions at the basis of this world and the intuitions still waiting for us to realize them. We already sense that the moment of *thanking* makes us intimate with the source of what is given.

The intensive practice of these more or less familiar features of the soul can lead us into unfamiliar territory. The various abilities in question (thinking, feeling, and so forth) can undergo a deep transformation. They can become as different from their undeveloped forms as risen bread is from flat dough. The exercises both secure our standing in the everyday world of work and play, of family and friends and colleagues, and also enliven the world beyond our normal experience. This is why I call it "the Stairway of Surprise." The phrase is from Ralph Waldo Emerson, the foundational American thinker, who wrote, "I shall mount to paradise/ By the stairway of surprise."[4] By deepening and purifying the ordinary functions of our hearts and minds, we can allow them to become surprising again.

While there is no predictable course to a surprise (or it wouldn't be one), Emerson could say something in advance about the overall direction: it is toward "paradise." By this Emerson meant to say that the qualities of wonder, love, and energy we normally put off until the hereafter can be found right here on Earth. Paradise is an earthly project. By intensifying and concentrating our soul, we draw the heavens and Earth together. We find occasions for wonder and surprise in the very fact of being here. These practices do not remove us from our obligations and relationships, but make us stronger so that we can perform them with delight. Spiritual traditions sometimes seem to give us tools to flee our life and work. Let it be stated at the outset that the tools offered here are meant as aids to incarnation. As Robert Frost wrote, "Earth's the right place for love. I don't know where it's likely to go better."[5] Love grows where there is both obstacle and potential, right here on Earth, in the midst of joy and misery.

I first encountered the six practices that make the steps of the Stairway in the work of Rudolf Steiner (1861–1925), the Austrian mystic and scientist who established Waldorf schools, biodynamic farming (an early organic method), and many other spiritually-based initiatives. Steiner called his approach to the spiritual life "Anthroposophy," the wisdom of the human being, and based his very practical inventions on what he called "spiritual-scientific research." This was a way of investigating what the world is and what it needs through a highly trained self-awareness. His views synthesized the spiritual traditions of the East (including ideas about karma and reincarnation) with those of the West (including Christianity) long before such syntheses were considered fashionable.[6]

Steiner placed great importance on these six practices, while presenting them in a slightly different form each time he invoked them. Somewhat misleadingly, Steiner called them "supplementary" or "subsidiary" exercises, since he meant them to accompany a central daily meditation. Yet these practices are deep meditations in themselves, and can stand alone. Steiner does not report how he derived the exercises; they have resonances in very ancient practices from the world's mystery traditions. For example, they overlap to some degree with the Buddhist idea of the six *paramitas*, or qualities of enlightenment. The qualities associated with the Hindu *chakras*, or energetic centers on the body, can also be seen as variants on the same themes. Rather than deriving their validity from tradition, however, in this book we will examine them on their own merits, as extensions of qualities we all know from everyday experience. They operate in the realm of the invisible, since they are forms of attention and they orient us toward understanding, both of which are invisible, primary phenomena.

In all their forms, such exercises rely on the insight that consciousness is real, not trivial, and that to improve our reality we must improve our consciousness. After all, we have no access to any world outside our consciousness; how could we? Steiner himself explored this terrain: in his early philosophical works, he emphasized the conceptual nature of what we perceive.[7] Yet our being limited by our consciousness, by how we see, turns out to be a moveable barrier that does not exile us from reality. By exercising our consciousness, we can shift the conceptual style by which we know the world. The *direction* of the shift we are seeking is easy to say — toward the source of all that is good — but not so easy to find and practice. If we do practice it, we find the world will change in three ways. First, we will perceive the world differently: it becomes more meaningful. Second, we will respond to this new world more creatively: we will add meaning to it. Third, meditation works directly in the invisible, and changes the world at its heart.

I met these six practices again in the work of Georg Kühlewind, a Hungarian chemist, psychologist, and linguist whose ideas have inspired much of what follows.[8] Similar ideas can be found here and there, in scattershot, throughout Emerson's *Essays*,[9] though it would have been most un-Emersonian for him to put them in order and suggest concrete exercises. Here I have gathered together and given new form to what I found above all in Steiner, in Kühlewind, and in Emerson.

These practices have been tested and applied in many ways. As chief psychologist in pediatric AIDS at Harlem Hospital in New York City, I practiced them intensively to cope with the extreme stresses of working with dying children and their families. As a husband and father, I have found them invaluable in addressing the conflicts, and augmenting the joys, of my own family life. As a psychologist in private practice, I have been able to guide some of my patients through the six exercises as part of their healing. As a conference and workshop leader, I have taught them to many hundreds. These experiences have convinced me that the Stairway can be helpful to anyone. Its steps are practical, and they find their most compelling application not only in retreat settings or in solitary meditative practice, but in our ordinary life.

To understand how the six steps of the Stairway work together, we need to return to the concept of the "extra" element in the human soul — that is, the capacity for attention that far exceeds what we need for material life alone. This something extra moves in one of two basic directions at any moment. It either traps us in habits (and self-orientation), or it turns into abilities (and freedom from fixed form). In one direction, it tends to solidify; in the other, it remains fluid. For most of us, the problem lies in the direction of solidity, of habit and the all-too-familiar. Usually it never occurs to us that the very consciousness with which we encounter life can shift, change, and develop new qualities. We assume that we already know how things are, to a very great extent, though it is just this "knowledge" of the world that has to be dissolved for fresh capacities to grow. As Will Rogers put it in his own down-home way: "It ain't what folks don't know that hurts 'em. It's what they know that ain't so."

Typically, we know far too much that ain't so. Well-padded by pseudo-knowledge, we pass right through the most brilliant intuitions, the most glorious showers and downpours of meaning, without suffering the tiniest insight. We stand in desperate need of surprise. Yet surprise will only become a steady feature of life if we school the functions of the soul so that they regain, even surpass, their original sensitivity and suppleness.

At every step of the Stairway, we immerse ourselves in a new beginning. It is good to recall that beginnings have always been celebrated, and to wonder why. We emphasize grace at the start of meals, the founding of a nation, the birthday of a child, the launching of a ship. Mystics have called their training "initiation" in reference to the life of constant beginning, of initiating, for which they educate their students. In the same way, we refer to the ceremonies at the end of a course of normal schooling as "commencement": the beginning rather than the end. Such rituals recognize the magic of the will to begin. Many traditions recognize the special faculty of openness in children ("except ye become as little children"; Matt. 18:3)[10] and suggest that we rediscover the openness of life's beginning in adulthood. Whenever we develop a talent, whenever we understand, whenever we give or forgive, we are engaged in the healthy employment of that human *extra* that otherwise ossifies into habit and prejudice. We *begin*.

The six exercises are to be practiced in succession: first the first, then the second, and so on. There are good grounds for the sequence given here, even though each supports and benefits from all the others.

Thinking comes first since it is at the basis of all we do: every decision and every act and every understanding. As the Buddha says, "We are what we think. All that we are arises with our thoughts. With our thoughts we make the world."[11] So thinking had better be the first of all the soul's functions to be transformed.

Otherwise our decisions about transforming the rest of our soul would themselves be carried out by an untransformed thinking, a bit like washing our hands with a bar of dirt instead of soap. *Thinking* takes us to the formless source of our thought's forms. The next step is *doing*, both a cure for the exhausted rush of daily life and a path into the sources of will. It teaches us to act out of a "soft" or meaning-oriented will, and even out of a spontaneous or empty will. The purifying of thought and will leads to exercises in purity of *feeling* — the kind of feeling that is also form-free, unstained by sympathy and aversion. Only an attention schooled to some degree in feeling can find the good in all situations, and so develop what is called *loving* on this Stairway. A predisposition toward the good keeps us well-oriented when we radically *open* to all that we encounter, free of words, concepts, and forms. *Thanking* is both end and beginning, both the result and precondition of the other steps. It propels us into a renewed ascent. (The Eightfold Path of Buddhism, which begins with right understanding, is usually depicted as a circle, which conveys this same idea of the end in the beginning, the beginning in the end.)

One possible way to proceed is to perform the first practice by itself, at least once a day, for a month. In the second month, you take up the second exercise intensively while continuing, in less intensive form, with the first. With each succeeding month you undertake the new exercise without losing the previous ones. By the sixth month, you are practicing *thanking* at least once a day, and each of the other five at least once a week. In this way, you can stay in touch with all of them and see how they reinforce one another. At the end of the first six months, you begin the round again.

Though the six steps can be differentiated conceptually, they are a continuum: perhaps this book should be called "The Waterslide of Surprise." Concentration in thinking, if it succeeds in purifying our thinking process sufficiently, leads us through all the "other" capacities. All lead to intensification of attention, so that the attention can exist one day without its theme and become the I AM experience.

As with physical exercise, you may notice that even when you sense that these practices are good for you, somehow it never seems like the right moment in the day to do them. You put them off until later, and then later you put them off again. Through the exercises themselves, this kind of avoidance eventually diminishes, but it may never quite go away. The domain of the habitual holds sway in us, and these exercises threaten it. They take some doing, whereas going on with life-as-it-is takes no effort at all (though it does consume our energy). They take some time, and while we always have time for our bad habits, it seems hard to "make time" for the good habits (though these *give* us energy). These exercises take much less time than we normally waste each day. Why not do them before rising from bed?

Though the exercises are in a sense "unnatural," since they require attention and intention, it is helpful to remember that they are not to be approached as work, but as play. It is up to you to find the best time of day to do them ungrudgingly. Do not think of them as laborious or even as important. You can go into them lightheartedly, with a relaxed body and an easy mind. Think of them not as one more added responsibility, but as refreshment. They will go much better if your attention to them is complete, and a cramped body or anxious mind will never allow you to focus complete attention. You want to get lost in the exercises as you get lost in a good book, forgetting even that you are reading. There is no effort then, and no concern or worry.

The question may arise, at different times and in different ways: "What are these exercises good for? Why do them at all?" To answer, we might consider the derivation of the English word *happy*. It comes from the same root as *happen*. To be happy is to be of the same substance as what happens. We participate in what fortune brings, and so we are fortunate. Instead of feeling separate or holding ourselves back from what is going on around us, we are *happy* when we co-create the events of the day. For most of us, this is far from our lived experience. We either look on passively or we rush around in self-centered activity. To take the middle route between these is to fully embrace and participate in what is happening. Yet this requires practice for most of us. It doesn't come naturally, but requires our creativity. The everyday powers of the soul that we take for granted can, in their developed, intensified forms, uncover our unity with all that is happening.

The six steps of the Stairway offer the most concrete routes to happiness in this sense. And while the exercises give us the strength to solve our practical problems, they also put us in a position to question and reframe our problems so that we experience them in a new light. From *thinking* to *thanking*, they all stand under the sign of beginning, and that means the end of comfort. Just as the *sadhus* of the Hindu tradition continually wander, allowing no attachment to place, the path of surprise keeps us from having a home in past habits. They upset everything in us that insists on the world as a dull round of sameness. To the extent, for example, that we nurse our grudges like gold, these exercises will threaten our treasure.

With a quality such as resentment, it is relatively easy to see that we have an unfortunate stake in keeping the world as it is, to our own and the world's ultimate disadvantage. It would be better, we would feel lighter, if we could forgive. The practices that follow question not only our resentments, but *all* the ways in which normal consciousness diminishes the world. For example, in the chapter on *opening* we will consider how normal sense-perception keeps us stuck; it is only one way of seeing things. We will consider methods of strengthening normal perception so that it puts us in touch with more of the world's expressiveness.

Most of the time, most of us don't really want the world around us suddenly to be more expressive. We want things to stay quiet and safe as we have always known them. Nor do we want suddenly to have more energy and power. We are quite content to complain. Don't worry! The practices suggested here will not hurl you into unmanageable and wild regions of experience. They *are* meant to give you new options, however. Normally, we are like pianists with arms tied to our sides, who can only reach and play the four notes on either side of middle C. The exercises given here are meant to release and extend your reach, so that there is a wider range of melody and harmony, and even dissonance, available to you.

The project of self-development in any form (religion, psychotherapy, "self-help") involves a measure of control. Instead of letting things happen, we take ourselves in hand and do something. Yet the exercises also require a special kind of allowing, a focused relaxation. For each exercise and at each moment, it is up to the practitioner to sense the specific balance of control and release that will lead to growth. In the ancient Celtic myth of Tristan and Iseult, Tristan puts himself in a boat with no oars or sails, and trusts the sea to take him on the right course. We too must actively choose our boat and our sea, but then there comes a moment in each exercise when we let the divine currents have their way with us. We find the point where "my" doing melts into the "world"'s doing, and at that moment the exercise becomes blessed.

Emerson knew that "the definition of *spiritual* should be, *that which is its own evidence*,"[12] and the Stairway of Surprise brings us into regions of self-evident clarity. We do not need external confirmation of our experiences, nor are we left guessing, but at certain blessed moments we can know for ourselves. "There is a depth in those brief moments," wrote Emerson in his essay "The Oversoul," "which constrains us to ascribe more reality to them than to all other experience."[13] The steps of this Stairway take us into increasing wonder, but also increasing sureness. They lead us out of mystification and into knowable mysteries. I sometimes hear people say, too easily, that this or that aspect of existence "cannot be known." But how do they *know* it cannot be known? One continuing surprise along the Stairway is that the world is knowable, understandable, from the roots to the twigs. On the one hand, we can come to know this or that more deeply: the sacred meaning, for example, that a stone "speaks" to us. On the other hand, we can sense at times that the world is not only knowable piecemeal, but that it is all of one piece, and the unity of the whole is also for us to understand.

It is possible that along the way, when you least expect it, in the midst of concentrating on something else, you become a Self — you awaken. This is the most important discovery possible. It arrives from just the opposite direction of those flattering experiences that supposedly build self-esteem. It comes when we forget ourselves, when we give ourselves, when we most wholly attend. Our normal sense of self lives by identifying with the body, with our personal history, and with our personal successes and resentments. The Self that lights up at moments of intense attentiveness needs no support of any kind. Just through this independent Self, we are capable of truly participating in our bodies, our past, and our relationships. An ancient Greek fragment runs, "I am a child of earth and the starry heavens." Through the awakening of our true Self (the awakening that *is* the true Self), we can know our dual heritage directly. As the Zen master Dogen wrote, "To study the Buddha Way is to study the self. To study the self is to forget the self. To forget the self is to be enlightened by the ten thousand things"[14] — precisely by what often seems so unenlightening.

The practices occupy only a few minutes a day. Yet they will inform and beneficially infect your other deeds through underground, hidden routes of unity, and not by your trying to spread the exercises out over the day. One of the sweetest surprises on the Stairway is that a little practice goes a long way. Its benefits permeate us without any effort. Who arranges for this to be so? Why do we get this undeserved reward? Emerson also wondered at such blessings. "A good deal of buzz, and somewhere a result slipped magically in."[15] This permeability of our souls to a little good practice is a foretaste of a larger wholeness. It refers from afar to the potential unity of all beings and times in a single point.

In my workshops, participants bring up all kinds of concerns. *I can't stop worrying. I can't stop crying. I'm always angry. If only we had children. I have nightmares. All my energy is gone. Should I leave my husband? She hurt me. I can't concentrate. He hurt me. I'm lost in life. They don't respect me anymore. What should I do about my career? I can't sleep. We don't trust each other.* These are just a few of the innumerable unfortunate forms the human *extra* can get trapped in. Often there is no single or simple solution. Yet there is a *turn* possible for everyone, a turn from suffering to creating. If they despaired absolutely that such a turn is possible, no one would go to workshops on the development of consciousness — nor would they pick up a book.

When I suggest practices from the Stairway of Surprise to my patients and workshop participants, it is because I know that the strength to grow through the most intractable problems can be developed on this path. Only a few people are willing to climb such a stairway. For those who do, it *always* helps. A stairway goes nowhere unless someone climbs it. And only you can begin.

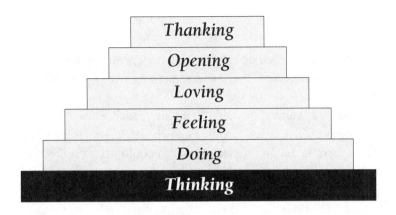

Thanking
Opening
Loving
Feeling
Doing
Thinking

Fortunately or not, everything we do is led by our thinking. There's just no way around it. Even if I say, "I'm going to stop thinking and let feeling be my guide" — that's a *thought*. Like the first step of a journey, it may pass unnoticed and forgotten, but you know it must have been there. If we are going to transform our basic capacities, we'd better begin with the most basic of all: the one that helps us choose and guide all others.

We may despise any reliance on thought as unromantic; we may suspect our thinking of being limited and culturally determined; we may complain of thinking as inadequate to its task of understanding this world and directing our behavior. What we can't do is avoid it. Each of these critiques is itself an example of thinking, and indeed dwells in an ocean of thinking. When we question thinking's authority, we haven't escaped it at all, since the process by which we could doubt it is (again) thinking itself.

A patient walked into my office one day and stewed in the juices of this problem for a few minutes.

"I'm sick of my whole mind," he said.

A lawyer, he relied on clear, critical understanding for his business life, and he knew there was something wrong with his very ability to think.

"I'm always angry," he said, "and I know it's because I'm always judging people. I mean, people do such stupid things. But criticizing them is making *me* sick. I wish I could get away from my thoughts and be at peace. We got back from vacation in Florida this week, and it was good in a lot of ways, but even when I'm fishing on a sunny day and everything's going well — the water is great, the boat is great, the fish are biting — still my mind is constantly racing and worrying. I might as well be at work. Then when I *am* at work, it's nothing but distractions. You know, when I was fresh out of law school I could focus on a brief or a letter or whatever it was and really get into it. Now my mind is either judging, worrying, distracted, or a little of each. I swear it would be better if I could just stop thinking altogether for a while. And here I am, criticizing myself too much! It just won't stop."

Eventually he came to see that what he really wanted was not *no* thinking, but more concentrated and livelier thinking. It wasn't so much that he wanted to shut his mind off. He wanted his mind to be clear. Instead of getting lost in anger and worry, he wanted to be able to focus. He sensed that his style of understanding had become both hardened and splintered when he needed it to be supple and whole.

Maybe our thinking, as much as our bodies, stands in need of exercise. We worry about our physical health, and spend fortunes to improve it, but do we ever apply that kind of self-improving zeal to our ability to think? Our minds, like our bodies, need a combination of flexibility and strength, qualities that are unlikely to return unless we do something.

While the lawyer put it in an unusually articulate way, many of my patients will simply complain of their inability to concentrate. Poor concentration is a psychiatrically recognized symptom of depression, attention-deficit disorder, schizophrenia, and many other problems. Even those of us who have not been diagnosed with such conditions may feel we cannot bring our minds to bear on anything with a sufficiently steady and receptive focus. Not surprisingly, we also don't find the answers to our questions.

Most of the time, most of what we call thinking is a maze of distractions. It could very well go like this: I want to decide about the kids' summer camp plans, and the brochure for one camp is in a folder on my desk. Summer camp is what I'm thinking about. But on the way to the desk I have to pass the fridge, and I recall that there's some good cheese in the cheese compartment. So I don't actually pass the fridge, I open it and take out a piece of cheese. I eat the cheese while pouring a glass of water. I swing away from the counter and remember I was going to phone my friend Tom. The phone is already in my hand when for a brief second I recall I was going to do something about the summer camp, but somehow I go ahead and dial Tom's number. By the time the call is finished, I have to race out the door to work, and the summer camp question is forgotten for another day.

This example shows how closely thinking and doing are intertwined. But it is always thinking that comes first: if my mind wanders, my behavior will wander too. The fridge is like a mousetrap, complete with cheese in it to catch the mouse. And there are many other kinds of traps and other kinds of cheese. Instead of being distracted by food, I might be taken away from thoughts of summer camp by a sequence of distractions that are themselves "thoughts": I begin to think of summer camp for my kids, then recall how much fun camp was when I went as a kid; then how I've lost touch with that guy Steve who was at Buck's Rock Camp; then I remember another friend named Steve, who played the violin; that leads to the image of my grandmother playing the piano, and then to worrying about tuning our own piano — and on and on and on, following the "cheese" into trap after trap. Soon I've forgotten what the original topic was at all. It takes me miles away from having a creative thought about sending my own children to camp.

The kind of jumpy sequence that takes me from memory to mental image to worry and around again is not thinking. It is what normally passes for thinking, but it is actually just a wandering around in associations. The notion that thinking is nothing *but* associations has only a brief history — since about the eighteenth century. Before that, people could distinguish thinking from its substitutes.[16] Even Freud, who didn't quite understand thinking, knew enough to marvel at our potential clarity of consciousness and creativity; he admitted that psychoanalysis was powerless to analyze the very ground of creativity and understanding.[17]

Thinking, whether clear or muddy, is not something added to our reality like a sprig of mental parsley adorning the main dish. It is what makes the substance of the world for us. We all know this in a general way, and most people can admit that they tend to live in a narrow zone of mental habits. But the role of thinking is more primary and pervasive than we generally realize. For what we call "reality" in normal consciousness — even the stuff of the world around us — is itself only our own past thoughts. Let me explain.

When we see a car, or an oak tree, or a cloud, we see them according to the thoughts we ourselves, and our whole society, have already thought about these things. In other cultures, dominated by other thoughts, they are seen differently. Adults teach them to children through language. The children learn these language-given concepts and see the world accordingly. There isn't any other reality for you than the concepts you have acquired or those you now acquire in the very act of perception.

Someone who has never learned the concept of writing will see a written page as a sheet of paper with black marks on it. We know that archaic cultures see the world differently. They live a reality largely alien to our own, shaped by thoughts we can only translate askew as we try to fit them into our standard assumption of a physical world "out there" with minds observing it. Analysis of the Homeric texts has shown that the ancient Greeks understood colors differently and therefore *saw* colors differently.[18]

When we dare to take this view seriously — and anthropology is full of examples to confirm it — we begin to realize that there is no world for us outside our thinking (or our past thoughts) about the world. Our very seeing, hearing, touching, and so on — the categories by which we anchor what is real to us — are permeated with concepts particular to our culture, language, and personal history. We will consider this in terms of meditative perception in the chapter on *opening,* but for now the essential feature is the conceptual nature of perception: we can see only what we can think.

Small children arrive without the fixed thoughts of a given culture, but are nevertheless oriented toward understanding. In the first few years of life they achieve what adults never do: the acquisition of a new language, complete with grammar and a perfect accent, but without any other, first language to translate from or use as a base of understanding. Adults learn a new language by the sweat of their brow, puzzling it out in terms of their first language. But children don't first learn to think (how would they?) and *then* learn their mother tongue. Instead they take in meaning and language at a single stroke, a single, coherent unit, from their human environment. For example, we never define a word like "but" to a child, nor could we. Yet the child learns to say and use the word "but" flawlessly, without ever puzzling it out in what we call thought. This will-to-meaning (as a contemporary Nietzsche might call it) is the greatest miracle, and holds the greatest promise for our view of human nature.

The good news, all but ignored in the psychology of childhood and the science of linguistics, is that human beings aren't neutral toward this world, but are originally tipped toward meaning, are pretuned to the melodies of significance. To some extent, linguists like Noam Chomsky have seen this: we have an innate drive toward language and meaning.[19] If it were not so, infants would never pay such attention to language, among all other sounds, and be accurately impressed by the meaning behind the words. They arrive already keyed to thinking, to understanding. They assume it is everywhere around them, and they actually discern what meanings are available to be feelingly understood in the minds of their human surroundings. They reach with their complete attentiveness past the sounds we make with our mouths to intuit the meanings behind the sounds. Their perfect confidence is that the world is understandable and the world is good. This is the certainty we see in the eyes of the very young — and it both inspires and shames us.

It shames us because we are so far from it. There is a moral quality to the intensity of absorption required for real thinking. Everything in us that is self-oriented, everything fallen and egotistical, involves a divergence from the free, true course of thinking in its clarity. Instead of being absorbed in the music we are playing at a concert, we worry about the audience's response: this is stage fright, and it is a lapse into self-orientation. Good music teachers always emphasize that the cure for stage fright is to become completely involved in the piece you are playing, although, in our fallenness, we may find this hard. T.E. Lawrence wrote that "happiness is absorption": I would add that when we are *not* absorbed, we tend to fall from happiness.

To receive meaning, children focus their whole being upon every utterance. Whatever they look at, whatever might mean something to them, fascinates them completely. Watch a group of children as they listen with open eyes and mouths to a good rendition of a fairy tale. They are literally in heaven, and nothing distracts them. The other day I saw an eight-month-old on her mother's lap in a restaurant, totally absorbed by the house guitar player. When the waiter dropped a tray nearby, all the adults turned toward the clatter of dishes, but the girl couldn't be swayed from her enchantment in the music. The child exhibits a depth of attentiveness so total she can not only disregard irrelevancies, but listening to a few hundred sentences she can receive a language's whole grammar and incorporate it into her soul.

By the age of reason (or at least by the age of financial worry), our minds have fragmented into what the Chinese call "the world of ten thousand things." At the same time, we begin to despair of ever understanding the world. Along with our capacity to be wholly attentive, we lose our original, childhood attunement to meaning. The less we can focus, the less we receive the significance of the world — like tired readers who see the words but no longer get the sense of the text. As Pascal said, "All human evil comes from this: man's being unable to sit still in a room."[20] We hasten through a senseless world with restless minds.

As a practicing psychologist, I see a great deal of suffering. Depending on your theory of psychology, you will tend to say the suffering is ultimately due to parental abuse, or to early childhood traumata, or to personality disorders, or to learned behaviors, or to dysfunctional cognitions, or to the workings of karma. Ultimately, it often seems to me, the worst suffering comes from *not under-standing*, and we all suffer from this ailment. Above all, there is the pain of not understanding what our life is for.

A recently widowed alcoholic asked me, while we stood over the deathbed of her only son as he lay dying of AIDS, "Why is *this* my life? Why is all this happening to me?" Her pain was not the pain of utter despair. If she'd really had zero expectation of the world, its senselessness would not bother her. No, such events bring suffering precisely because, beneath our surface despair and even indifference, we know that we *could* understand and make meaning. "We grant that human life is mean," writes Emerson, "but how did we find out that it was mean? What is the ground of this uneasiness of ours, of this old discontent? What is the universal sense of want and ignorance but the fine innuendo by which the soul makes its enormous claim?"[21]

Certainly there is no fixed formula that would mean much to this grieving mother. If anything could satisfy her longing for meaning, it wouldn't be a dead thought, but only an intuition that *is* an intuition for her. Emerson, who had his share of personal tragedies, also knew this problem.

"Thought is the manna that cannot be stored," wrote Emerson, referring to the special bread the Lord provided for the Jews in their forty years of wandering in the Sinai.[22] They were allowed to eat every morning where they found this fresh white stuff, but not to keep any of it against the future. When they tried, it turned putrid and worm-infested (Exod. 16:12–20). Thinking itself is a manna of magical nourishment, though it satisfies us only in the instant of its creation. A nanosecond later, and the understanding has fled. It dies into the words by which we formulate it, and which no longer hold it. "Understanding comes in mid-sentence," wrote the sixth-century Zen sage Bodhidharma; "what good are doctrines?"[23] The kind of understanding that could satisfy our hunger for meaning, even in the face of life's tragedies, would not be the supposed thinking we rightly condemn as cold, dead, and alien to life. It would be thinking itself: a presence that cannot be stored, yet whose immediacy can answer any question.

At one point in Shakespeare's play, the young Hamlet observes his evil uncle Claudius at prayer. He resolves that he will not kill Claudius just now (and so avenge his father's death) precisely because Claudius is communing with the divine. Hamlet wants to wait and kill him later, when his sins are upon him, "in th'incestuous pleasures of his bed" — so as more effectively to send him to hell.[24] Whatever we think of Hamlet's vengefulness, he's quite wrong about Claudius's prayer. As Claudius himself mutters under his breath, his soul is not in fact being purified, nor is his conscience clear, because he cannot really *think* his prayer with his whole self. Instead, it is the kind of "thinking" that has died into its verbal expression. It is *merely* words, a kind of mental chaff. As he complains to himself, "My words fly up, my thoughts remain below. Words without thoughts never to heaven go."[25]

Unlike our relatively deadened verbal consciousness, actual thinking is alive. Like children, we each have a perfect confidence that this essential thinking is infallible. Like children, we don't (and can't) fundamentally doubt it. The thinking that precedes the words, the thinking that comes before the images and gives rise to them, the *source* of what we normally call thinking — just that is what I mean by *thinking* here. It is the source of all our intuitions.

As adults, we are condemned to start our schooling of consciousness at the other end of the process from the Israelites. Instead of beginning with the pure manna of thinking, we must start with thinking in its normal, decayed form. We can't just declare our way into a fantasied clarity and fluidity of thought. We can only start with the here and now. We begin our journey, along with Yeats, "where all the ladders start / In the foul rag-and-bone shop of the heart."[26] That is, we begin with fallen thinking, distractions, prejudices and all, and wrestle our way back to thinking in its clear formlessness (though our best wrestling move is *not to struggle*).

For the miracle performed by children is still available. Just as a child can learn any language effortlessly at birth, in our healthier moments we are open to any kind of insight. We can learn something new and solve all problems. Thinking itself, coursing just beneath our welter of mental habits, has no fixed forms. Nothing traps it. When we find this generative clarity at the roots of thinking, we can recognize it as superior to any given thought, for it is the giver of thoughts. Our thinking loses its dry, abstract quality and begins to irradiate us with new life. Emerson: "Shakespeare carries us to such a lofty strain of intelligent activity, as to suggest a wealth which beggars his own."[27] We feel we are at the fruitful, fecund source.

Thinking itself goes on unconsciously, and what normally emerges into consciousness is the already-thought, the finished thing that is a result of that hidden process. We are not awake in the moment of understanding itself. We sleep through the real action, and wake up to see its result. We always arrive on the scene of consciousness a moment too late.

This is simple to see. Think of a color. Go ahead: think of a color now.

Well? A color just came to you. It arrived as if prechosen. You weren't awake at the moment of choice, the moment of thinking through *which* color to pick. (Or if you chose between two, you were not aware of the moment of coming up with those two to choose from.) Finished concepts arrive in consciousness, the results of an invisible process.

Every thought is like this. By the time we have it in awareness and can observe it, it is *already thought*. When this becomes clear, it prompts a simple, difficult question: where is the living source itself? Where is thinking, where is understanding and choice, *before* it has died into normal consciousness? For that is the thinking that is free of distraction, even the distraction of having-already-been-thought, and that is the thinking that could link us back to the world from which we feel so separate.

We always rise on our Stairway of Surprise by a practice of *intensification*. Just by deciding to do so, we can select a theme to think about and then begin to think it more slowly, more clearly, more deeply than we do in normal waking life. Instead of thinking for the sake of an immediate practical result, we can think as art for art's sake: a kind of play. In this way, we can be more wholly present in our own minds. As we do, we come to live less in thinking's products and more in its processes. We begin to live in the light, rather than in what it strikes.

To discover thinking at its source, it is helpful to begin with a single theme that we try to think exclusively. This will reveal how strong (or weak) our concentration has become.

Distractions from thinking are fascinating liars. They don't announce themselves as distractions at all. They slink into consciousness, wolves in sheep's clothing, disguised as our very own thoughts. Having tried to focus on a phrase from the Scriptures or the Sutras, we soon find ourselves wondering about lunch. Or we may be distracted by a loud noise, or some sharp regret, or a bodily ache. There is no moment when anyone deliberately says, "I'll take a break from 'God is love' to nurse a few grudges." Instead the grudges, or the idea of lunch, or remembering something I need to do later today, just slink in as "my" thought, and seduce me away from the topic at hand.

Sooner or later I may wake up from my distraction. I may realize, "Oops! What's this? Why am I thinking about lunch? What was I doing? Oh, yes: 'God is love.'" Having awakened, I now have a choice. I can return to the original theme, or I can go on to something else.

This amounts to a four-part process: focusing, distraction, waking up, and refocusing. It gives the structure of the normal, failed act of attention. With practice, it can run through its paces differently and so stay nearer to the theme. Practice deepens the process at every stage: I can stay with the theme longer before wandering. I can awaken from wandering more quickly. I can refocus more wholeheartedly. All exercises of consciousness, not just thinking, depend on our continually improving our relationship to distractions.

Several insights emerge from trying to think about a simple subject even for a few minutes — whether about a fork or a biblical theme or an event in life. For one thing, we notice that our distractions are never creative. They are all about "me" in one way or another — what I already want or dread. They never really break new ground.

The more lightheartedly I can concentrate, on the other hand, the more creative my thinking becomes — it feels fresher and more alive, and intuitions (that is, understandings close to their source) arrive with greater frequency. Concentration is really improvisation. If I am truly absorbed in my theme, I will not think the same thing about it as I did yesterday — or, if I do, I don't notice. Any memories of what I have already thought, like familiar ideas about the object from other sources, are just distractions.

The theme itself turns out to be alive and changing, instant by instant, if I can keep with it.

At a certain intensity of thinking, it becomes clear that my thoughts are both something I produce and something that is already "there." On the one hand, I have to do it if there is to be any thinking; it is my own deed. On the other hand, it seems that my simple orientation toward the theme brings forth ideas I didn't create: they arrive from somewhere.

The Practice of Thinking

Take a man-made object as your focus. It could be a fork or a shovel or a saltshaker: something simple and thoroughly understandable to you — not a complicated device. You sit in any position that keeps you as awake as possible, and simply turn your mind to the object. Begin to get interested. Think about it in words or in images, or else alternate between these styles — one day more in images, the next day more in words.

You may notice that your thinking is hasty. That is, you may feel "done" with the theme very quickly, and then you need more content to work with. As thinking intensifies, it also slows down. You eventually find you can dwell with an apparently simple theme free from any sense of rush or "already being done." This shift is aided by thinking more in pictures than in words. The exercise stops being a chore and becomes enjoyable, light. Distractions happen less often, they take you less far away from the theme, and you wake up from them more quickly.

Don't change your object, but keep thinking about the same one for many days (you can do it fruitfully for years and decades). If you manage to stay with a fork, neither bored nor distracted, for ten minutes at a stretch on the four-hundredth trial of this exercise, you will have developed a strong attentional style. By then you will have noticed that at other moments too, quite apart from the exercise, you can stay with a theme — for instance, a theme in conversation or a work problem that needs to be solved — more fruitfully.

One useful trick in concentrating on the mental picture of a man-made object is to mentally address it: "How do you look?", "Don't go away!", etc. This practice keeps our will "soft" and feeling-oriented rather than objectifying the object.

There are many benefits to concentration on a man-made object, including the fact that the object is initially uninteresting, so that it requires an intense concentration to stay with it for any length of time. We discover, perhaps with horror, how weak our concentration is. Yet *whatever* you intentionally focus on will help all your subsequent acts of attentiveness. As Simone Weil wrote in her sparkling essay "Reflections on the Right Use of School Studies with a View to the Love of God": "Even if our efforts of attention seem for years to be producing no result, one day a light that is in exact proportion to them will flood the soul. Every effort adds a little gold to a treasure no power on earth can take away."[28]

When a distraction takes you away from the theme, at some point (as we discussed above) you will wake up to the fact that you are distracted. You wonder, "How did I get here?" — and you find yourself anywhere from summer camp to tuning the piano. It is helpful at such times to return to the chosen theme by working back, but now intentionally, along the course of associations that were unintended when they distracted you. Something unusual happens through this practice. You find you were "there," present, during the associations that passed like a dream. A hidden witness was awake even while you were asleep. Initially we only sense this hidden witness through such moments of reviewing distractions. It comes to full self-awareness in the course of further practice, when it can emerge as the I AM or true Self — the awakening.

Practice with a man-made object gradually brings to light *how* we think — the form or governing style of thinking that is normally hidden from consciousness and available only in its results. Steiner said that our normal thinking, in which we notice first one thought, then the next, then the next, is something like a person coming upon a field strewn with corpses that must once have been alive.[29] By concentrating intensively, we meet these folk before their death: we discover thinking in its still-living process. We even see them die. That is, we can survey the change, repeated continually, from living, thinking process to dead, discrete, "normal" thoughts.

The object of focus here consists only apparently in a thing, a physical object. Concentration reveals that it is ultimately an idea (the functional idea of the object) that stands behind all examples and mental pictures of the object. We normally understand this idea in a practical way, since we always know what functions as a fork, for instance, no matter how it looks, and yet we never have it clearly in consciousness under normal circumstances. By concentrating, we can approach this source point. Where we initially only *have* an idea, gradually we ourselves *become* the idea. Such an exercise prepares us to find the inside, the meaning side, of every phenomenon.

Further practice in thinking moves beyond *concentration* to *meditation*. Where concentration involves focusing on a theme we already know, meditation presents us with themes we do not know but must find — and the process of discovering such themes has no endpoint. One form of meditation that has been used in many traditions is to take a passage from a sacred text — the Bible, the *Bhagavad Gita*, the sermons of the Buddha — and allow the motivating idea of the passage to be your primary focus. You might take the theme, "The tree of eternity has its roots in heaven and its branches reach down to the earth."[30] You think about it, drawing all your powers of attention to the text. This will include pondering over other things you've heard about it, perhaps, and whatever you know about the author or context of the passage. Thinking circles closer and closer to the theme. As it does, the theme changes.

In this practice, too, words and images are where you begin. They articulate your orientation to the theme. Yet you do not simply repeat the words of the sentence over and over: such repetition tends to make the theme less, rather than more, meaningful. Instead, as with the man-made object, by pondering on the theme you begin to sense that all the ideas about it that arrive in your mind, clothed in words and images, come *from* somewhere.

As thinking intensifies, these ideas from the source start to enter consciousness with a sense of greater authority. They mean more. They begin to rain down on you in richer profusion. With mounting interest, all else disappears. The theme alone is alive. That sense of reality you normally only invest in your own body and life transfers itself to the theme. You feel, with a kind of inner astonishment, *this is real; this is true*. You are completely unconcerned with the success or failure of the exercise, and oblivious to whether you are thinking in words or not, since only the theme exists. Distance disappears, and you become the very source of the theme, which is boundless.

At this point, every understanding is available to you.

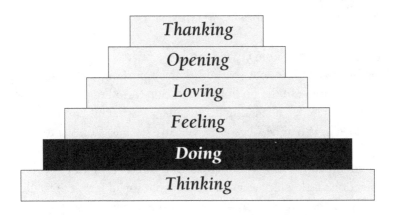

Long ago, the Apostle Paul complained bitterly about his inability to do what he really wanted. He put the thing as simply as it could be put: "The good that I would, I do not; but the evil which I would not, that I do" (Rom. 7:19). Two thousand years later, almost everyone I know is caught in the same bind.

Whether it is a diet we can't stick to, a habit we can't shake, or a job we don't put ourselves out for, it seems we all succumb. We are inconstant — and not through any lovely spontaneity. For most of us, it would be more astonishing to be steadfast and constant in our actions than to be new and different. Or rather, keeping our word *is* the new and different style we need for most of our actions.

In my psychotherapy practice I see many forms of this inconstancy. One patient feels stymied by his hypercritical boss and backbiting colleagues; he wants to leave and may soon be fired, but he can't seem to look for a new job. It's as if the phone weighs a thousand pounds; he just won't make the calls he needs to make. Another patient, a mother and single parent, keeps signing her child up for too many classes and activities; she knows she's overburdening him, but she finds herself pushing him to achieve more and more to the point of exhaustion. Another patient keeps losing his temper, alienating his friends, his wife, his children, his employees. When he "sees red," he can't seem to stop the torrent of abusive language, the violent gestures, that follow. All these are good people, insightful people, and often very strong people. They don't lack willpower. They lack what we all lack: the faculty of *doing*, the capacity to live and move from out of our best intuitions.

One young woman came into every session to complain about her boyfriend, and she did have things to complain about. One week I heard he was messy around the house. The next week he was using "too much" cocaine. He wouldn't look for a job. He hit her. He started dealing cocaine. He was seeing other women. Yet when I wondered out loud about this fellow's suitability as a marriage prospect, my client was way ahead of me. "Oh," she said, "I know I should leave him. Right away. Or yesterday! I hate him. I just can't seem to get out the door, though."

We spent some months chewing on that favorite bone of psychotherapists, the past. What about her abusive father? Was she angling to fulfill unmet dependency needs? One day she was telling a story from her childhood, and I was listening empathically, when she suddenly interrupted herself with a realization that completely changed how she saw her problem. "Know what?" she said. "It's not my past. It's me. If I'm ever going to leave him, *I* have to do it." She invented for herself the antidote to St. Paul's problem.

There are times when it is helpful and right to explore the past.

As young children, we drink up our environment in deep drafts, and then spend much of adulthood spewing it out again. "Give me a child until the age of seven," goes the Jesuit boast, "and I'll give you a Catholic for life." Our early environment schools us in the ways of relating, ways of being, ways of doing that later seem to come most naturally. And when these ways are crooked, we may limp for life. Children vary in their reactions to childhood trauma, as to childhood blessings, yet the past does matter.

Still, if *everything* in us is from the past, we might as well throw out any project of self-improvement — in fact, any project at all. For if we were completely filled up with the past, there would be no room in us for something or someone that could do something about the past. Whenever we think that in fact we can change anything in us, even a little bit, we are declaring our faith in a capacity for newness that nothing can altogether spoil — not the future with its fates, the present with its tortures, or the past with its ghosts.

This freshness may be hidden under a lot of mulch, but as long as we are human it cannot completely disappear. Psychological theories that we human beings are "nothing but" this or that — nothing but our biology, nothing but our brain functioning, nothing but trained behaviors, nothing but learned cognitions — are both pessimistic and self-contradictory. Yet those are the mechanistic, deterministic theories that rule our science and medicine.

Such theories overlook what the Greek mythic and philosophic tradition called our "fire," our portion of the "first fire." Such theories are pessimistic, despite all their promises of progress, because they say in effect there is nothing we can do ourselves. If they were taken seriously, there could be no laws. Who is a criminal, if we have no responsibility for our actions? My past made me do it. My brain made me do it. My early training made me do it. My genes made me do it. And who has ever been good? By these theories, no one.

Our conviction that there is something uncrushably good, uncrushably responsible, in the human being not only allows us to convict criminals of their crimes (because they could have done otherwise), it also teaches us mercy toward them (because they could improve again).

When my son Asher was five, we were driving through our Brooklyn neighborhood one day and saw a public-service billboard warning against drunk driving. It showed several crash dummies in a car, their mechanical heads rammed through the windshield glass. The caption said something about how stupid it is to drink and drive. Asher asked me what those robots in the picture were, and I told him they were a kind of statue normally used to test car safety. You can send them through a car crash to see what would happen to a human body in a crash like that, but without hurting anyone.

Asher thought for a moment.

"Why don't they just use villains?" he said. "It would show what really happens in a crash."

That set me back. Why *not* just use villains?

"Well," I answered slowly, "even if someone has done something really bad, even if someone is a terrible criminal, there is generally a corner in them that is good. Most criminals aren't completely bad. So I guess that's why you can't just use them like crash dummies and kill them to test car safety."

Asher wasn't put off for long.

"Why not use the villains that *are* completely bad?" he said.

At this point I got that feeling other parents have reported to me about being with their own children: the feeling of losing ground against a strong legalistic mind trapped in a five-year-old's body. I wasn't prepared in the moment to tell Asher that no one is completely bad. What I could, and did, say was that though some people might be completely bad, there is no way to tell for sure. You don't want to use criminals as crash dummies in cars, because you just might make a mistake: *there might still be someone inside the villain.* Asher could go along with that.

For the difficulty St. Paul named — that we don't do as we want, that we do as we *don't* want — only represents the dark side of human doing. He was lamenting the difficulty we have in performing our intuitions. There's a bright side, too, of course: when a human being perfectly obeys, through the body, the inner promptings of the spirit. From the catalogue of glorious human achievements that could draw our attention, such as the political leadership of Gandhi, the musicianship of Yo-Yo Ma, or the deep act of religious ritual, perhaps the brightest may be a kind of doing we each perform every day: speaking.

We don't need a more glamorous model. What happens during speech is the great miracle, and if we could do *that* consciously, in all our actions, we would be home free. Instead of solving the problem of effective action by talking about strength and willpower, about self-esteem and goals, let's talk about this most effortless, this lightest of actions, and take the lessons it has to offer.

Language has magic to it. It is no wonder that magical formulas often consist of incantations, spells, and other forms of doing by speaking. Many traditions describe the first work of the universe, the creation of the world, as an act of speech: the Word in the beginning, the Lord's "Let there be light." Important moments in our lives are marked by speech that has a special efficacy to it. When the mission controller says, "Lift off!", when the bride says "I do," it is not just information but a *deed*.[31] Everything good that comes about in human life comes about through the word, whether it is spoken or not. Every road that is built, every meal that is cooked, every grain that is grown — it all takes place through what human beings have said or meant. Like words, all our true deeds give perceptible clothing to what is originally invisible and inaudible: the idea.

Turning the focus of attention onto our own bodies, we can notice that our slightest act of speech represents the same magic in miniature. For we merely conceive the idea, like God before the world began, and the tongue, lips, voice box all operate in concert to carry it out. It is creation from nothing every time. You decide to speak, and the body moves.

You may object, "The brain is making the body move." You may think, "Surely it's a matter of muscles and nerves." But none of the recent research in brain plasticity supports the materialist notion that the brain thinks or that the body controls itself. Just the reverse. The brain does nothing on its own. *You* have to tell your brain what to do. And when you do so, it not only obeys but knits itself anew according to your thoughts. In violinists, the portion of the brain's motor cortex that corresponds to the left fingers (whose busy action makes the notes) is physically bigger than that of non-string players. The brain doesn't force the violinist to play that sonata; instead the violinist's playing shapes her brain.[32]

When you speak, you do not normally think about *how* to speak. You just focus on what you want to say and say it. You trust that the language and your body will do their work. Before uttering your sentence, you don't worry about the grammar. None of us speaking our mother tongue thinks, "Now, where should I put the direct object of the verb?" Nor do we worry about sound production. No one with normal speech function thinks, "How should I place my tongue to get the 'T' sound in 'technology'?" We merely conceive our idea, decide to speak, and then coast flawlessly into the act of speech with the ease of a gliding swan.

What would it be like to have one's whole life work this way? What would it be like to lead a wordlike life? That is the issue. For when we are inconsistent, when we have the plan to stop smoking and don't carry it out, then we are falling into something like a lapse of grammar. Our actions no longer convey our best meaning. We are failing, as the saying goes, "to keep our word." But when our intuitive thinking coincides with our doing, when our bodies and thoughts work in concert, then we enter life surprisingly. For then, in a single act, we can conceive a leap and leap it.

In 1919 Steiner was asked to give advice to teachers about how to teach children in kindergarten, and he said their willpower would develop in the right way if they engaged in "meaningful actions."[33] He went on to define which actions could be called meaningful: they are actions undertaken for others. So when the children in a Waldorf school bake bread, they bake it for the class as a whole. A child doesn't knead the little lump of dough for himself or herself alone. This is meaningful action, and it is an act of speech. It says something.

Just as thinking is always correct (if it really is thinking), so doing is always good (if it really is doing). Meaningful action is moral action. We have the true thought, then carry it out as the good deed — which is why we had to look at thinking first. Until our thoughts are clear, whatever we do will tend to be the dupe of our distractions, and the monkey body will swing wildly after the monkey mind. Once our thinking deepens, approaching its deep source, our deeds will also be blessed.

In the Middle Ages, great religious figures like Nicolas of Flue in Switzerland often praised "obedience" as the highest virtue. When I was a teenager, such a notion would have seemed utterly abhorrent, evoking images of groveling dependence on authority figures and the established order — and that is how obedience has often been (mis)understood. But now I can guess at a different quality that may have been the original meaning of *obedience*, a word derived, after all, from the Latin for "hearing." The point may not originally have been to bow to the Church or the Temple elders, but to hear the guidance of the spirit — whether it appears as a burning bush, an angel's revelation, or the simple promptings of an accurate conscience. Once you have the certainty of the true thought and the right way, then nothing should prevent you from acting in accordance with your understanding (unless you realize you were in error). *That* is obedience. Every action could be as obedient to our intuitions as the speech organs are to our thoughts.

Sometimes this kind of doing happens best in disasters. The intensity of a fire or flood can concentrate and enliven us so that we see clearly and act directly. It is a miracle of its own, known as presence of mind. I remember one sultry summer's day in Brooklyn when I saw a man run out of a store and tear down the street.

An instant later, another man holding a bar of iron came charging out of the store screaming, caught up with the first guy, and began to swing the bar in his face. He was in a white-hot rage. A passing student saw what was happening, strode up to grab the bar of iron, spoke one or two words of calm, and took the bar so fluently from the pursuer's hand that he hardly resisted. Some tense moments followed, but the store owner and thief worked it out with the police. No one got hurt.

I lingered when it was all over to ask the student what he'd done. "Oh," he said, "I did what anyone would do. I kind of saw my chance and took it." He himself didn't recall the calming words he'd spoken to the store owner. Word and deed were one.

When we practice *doing*, we learn to make presence of mind our daily habit. We exchange a life of senseless repetition for one of significant improvisation — that is, acting with presence of mind, free from any sense of constraint. Doing becomes our speech. We can learn, at least occasionally, to act out our intuitions with the same effortlessness by which we utter words in our mother tongue.

One school-day morning, I was trying to pry my six-year-old son Rody out of his bed. With my every coaxing word and my every tug at his blankets, he wormed his way deeper under the sheets. Then I remembered the principle of *doing as speech*, and I found a way to get him up.

"Work consists of anything a body is obliged to do," as Tom Sawyer understood, while play is what we put meaning into effortlessly. So I decided to tell Rody a story, and just to get his attention I told it about someone else who had trouble getting out of bed: Rip Van Winkle. He had such a hard time, he slept for twenty years. When he finally did wake up, his beard stretched down to his toes. And so on. The moment Rody heard that a story was afoot, he perked up. He sat bolt upright in the bed and began asking questions, while I easily helped him to dress. We decided to act out parts of Rip Van Winkle's story together, and suddenly the project of getting up became a brief and insignificant obstacle to our play.

The Asian martial arts sometimes use a similar technique. Your opponent is grimly engaged in a fight, which is all about pushing and hurting (fundamentally meaningless), while you put yourself in a more truly powerful position by moving your arms as if shooing crows off a cornfield (or whatever). That is, you put yourself in a meaning-making frame of mind. You move your body to *signify*, to *mean*, and not to exert power. This realm is connected, too, to the oft-noticed capacity of stutterers to speak fluently when they get angry or when they speak a foreign language. The special condition of anger or of French distracts them for a brief time from the accustomed and painful effort of trying to enunciate clearly — and clear speech is the result.

The Practice of Doing

How can you bring this magical aspect of doing into your own life? The first practice is to pretend your way into what Kühlewind calls the "soft will," which is the will by which we speak. For example, while walking to the store, or while raking leaves, or while doing the dishes, or while entering dates in your organizer, you can make the activity part of a "role," part of an inner dialogue or game. You may imagine that the cup from the water cooler contains a single dose of the elixir that will cure any illness, and you debate inwardly whether to take it yourself or give it to someone else. You may imagine that every step on the way to the bus stop is between peonies you don't want to crush, or on a tightrope high above a crowded circus tent. Whether this makes a difference will depend on how thoroughly you imagine the scene. If you succeed in enjoying the exercise, you will notice that the outward event (doing the dishes) is lightened. It becomes less of a burden, and accomplishes itself as if on its own.

I met an old Dutch gentleman whose father had been a blacksmith. I asked if his father sang while he worked. Yes, my friend told me, he sang some, but above all he beat the anvil *in rhythm*, which made the day go by with no weariness. His "work" strokes were part of the rhythm rather than the other way around.

The intention in such exercises is simply to enter the realm of imaginative doing, and so to change the quality of the experience from our normal emphasis on usefulness to a more unusual emphasis on meaning, on telling a story with our deeds. Even a momentary immersion in role playing or song will convince you that it changes the quality of the experience.

A further practice of doing consists in performing, as if in slow motion, a simple movement that you decide to undertake for no utilitarian reason. For example, you can open a book and close it without reading a word. Every tiniest gesture, from first reaching for and touching the cover to letting it fall closed again, should be undertaken in a state of complete yet relaxed alertness. What we normally do with our mind racing to its ten thousand preoccupations we now do in total concentration. For the period of exercise, we follow our own doing with our thinking alertness. If the mind wanders, we just bring it back to the task at hand. This form of doing is not unlike the Buddhist practice of mindfulness, and has many of the same benefits.

You may notice that it is hard to "catch" the very first instant of an intentional movement. It is no easy task to supervise, in perfect awareness, that split second at which you first make your hand budge to reach for the watering pot. You may find that the will itself is invisible to you, while the thought ("I'll reach for the book now") and the perception (you see your fingers touch the cover) are easily observable. It is also hard to notice the last instant of your chosen action. All too easily, you find you have already finished and somehow you weren't "there" at the moment of stopping. Yet it is possible to be right there.

You can intensify the moment of beginning by inserting a pause between the decision and the first physical motion to carry it out. The question of *how* we do anything, how the thought translates into action and how the action comes to an end, can become an astonishing puzzle to you. No tale of nerve impulses and brain events will solve it, since it is a question of consciousness, while the brain and nerves are *in principle* inaccessible to direct experience. As we discussed before, recent developments in the science of brain plasticity continue to show that the brain does what *you* tell it to do, not the other way around. So the miracle of how we decide and will and do persists, no matter whether we look at the moving hand or at the brain and nerves. We have the idea, and somehow we start; we have the idea, and somehow we stop.

Following up your astonishment by paying ever-closer attention to the actions themselves, you may find that you are led into an unusual sense of achievement. You begin to guess at the sources of the will. You experience the abundant privilege of movement, a kind of movement that is not of your body alone. You feel that the slightest deed is resonant, suggestive, and connected to the world about you in ways that were previously unguessed. The locus of control, the source of the movements, shifts from inside your skin to "outside," or to no spatial location at all. The Zen saying, "I lift my little finger and cover Mount Sumeru," may abruptly shift from an obscure paradox to a self-evident statement of fact. You raise an eyebrow and encompass the globe.

Such experiences stand on their own and justify themselves. You don't feel the need for them to be of use for anything else. In fact, the feeling that the experience is complete in itself shows that you are practicing to good effect. You will experience as very striking the difference between a sweat-of-your-brow approach to this practice and the moments when it becomes a more effortless involvement.

The tendency of the Stairway as a whole, and of doing in particular, is to plunge you more directly into the fulfillment of your day-to-day chores. It makes light of life's burdens. As doing takes hold, you may be no less busy, but in moments of grace you will know, beyond all utility, what you are busy *for*.

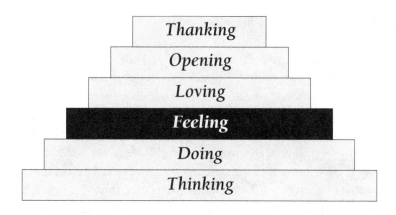

| Thanking |
| Opening |
| Loving |
| **Feeling** |
| Doing |
| Thinking |

A couple has come to see me because the husband is always angry at his wife.

Jack has a sense of being unloved by Annette, of being neglected. He is jealous of everyone she talks to, jealous of her time in the bathroom, jealous of her time in the supermarket. He has been known to fly into rages over this feeling of neglect, yelling abuse and even throwing furniture. It is painful to see his anger at her, partly because it is so self-defeating. The more he rages against her abandonment, the further she retreats. After eighteen years of marriage, with constant hectoring from him, Annette is on the point of packing her bags. If it weren't for the children, she would have left long ago. When we talk about ways for the two of them to communicate better, they won't budge from their fixed positions: "She doesn't love me." "He wants too much closeness." It's a theme they play over and over, with few variations.

As we talk about their early life together, before this problem emerged, just by chance we start to focus on a new topic. In the early days, Jack wanted to be a professional violinist. He had won some competitions. He had had some solo concerts. He had nearly gotten a recording contract. But things in the music world soured for him, and he had become a building contractor instead. I ask him about those early years and what it was like to be part of the professional musicmaking world. As he speaks about it — the impromptu concerts with friends, the life of constant practicing, the excitement of concert performance, the late Beethoven quartets he loved — Jack changes. His face, how he holds his body, the tone of his voice, all reveal something I've never seen before, and that Annette says she hasn't seen in many years. It is his deep love of music. As he speaks, the very air in the office seems cleaner, the space in the office seems roomier. He begins to cry softly. They go home and have the best week (and the best sex) of their married life.

What is happening here? In my language, Jack has emerged from the prison of *emotion* (his anger) and entered a world of real *feeling* (his sense for music and love).

Emotions are about the separate self. It is always "*my* anger" or "*your* anger"; it is always "*she* is jealous" or "*he* is worried." The inner experience we call emotion is literally self-ish: it is about our own selves. When we die, our emotions die with us. They aren't integral to the world that provokes them. The oak in the yard will remain after I die; my pleasure in the oak perishes with me.

Feeling is something else again. Like emotion, feeling is also an inner and lively experience, but unlike emotion it is an experience of a truth that will survive me rather than a report on my personal inner weather. It is not a cold, abstract experience of truth, but — well, a *feeling* experience of truth. All the juice, the liveliness of emotions is still present, but now it is no longer preoccupied with the person doing the feeling. Sensitivity has turned outward, toward life. Instead of feeling myself, I feel *that* — something beyond me. So we speak a greater truth than we know when we say our "feelings" have been hurt. More than hurt: by our whole stance in the world, our capacity to feel has been shifted and twisted; it has soured and turned self-ish. It has become *mere* emotion.

Emotion-lovers will bridle at this characterization, and I have overstated it somewhat to make the point strongly. In fact our inner lives are neither angel food cake nor devil's food cake, but marble cake — a swirl of emotion and feeling in which one often blends into the other. The spontaneity and warmth of the inner life are not going to be sacrificed here to some chilly ideal. We are all familiar with emotional experiences that are already feeling, or on the borders of feeling: wonder, curiosity, interest, compassion, devotion. Our better destiny does have a direction, and it is toward a more feeling encounter with the world.

The view that problematic qualities in the soul are decadent versions of something finer crops up in many traditions. Bodhidharma said that the goal of development was to go from the Buddhist "three poisons" of greed, anger, and delusion "back to morality, meditation, and wisdom."[34] The seven deadly sins and seven virtues of Catholicism present a similar pairing. (I learned this distinction between emotion and feeling from Kühlewind.)[35]

Daniel Goleman has written about "emotional intelligence," contrasting it with verbal intelligence.[36] Actually, though, the life of feeling is at the source of *all* intelligence. From our first understandings to our greatest intuitions, experiences of truth are always experiences of feeling. Logic, too, is based on feeling — the feeling for evidence, for what "makes sense." This is how we know that a syllogism or proof "works": by our accurate feeling. Once again, it is not a self-oriented feeling, but a feeling for what is really there. It can be confirmed by others who have a similarly developed clarity of feeling. To see this is to begin to understand that the human being is not an arbitrary bundle of separate functions, but a rainbow of related capacities. Our feeling, thinking, and willing are the variegated hues of a single original light.

If we think back to Jack and Annette, we can get further clues about how the self-oriented quality of emotion works. Jack's anger at Annette is based on ancient habits of mind, dating back at least to the time when his parents abandoned him in early childhood (he was raised in a foster family). His sense of being hurt, of Annette leaving him constantly, certainly seems accurate and real to him. Yet observers from the outside would agree (and do) that at such times he is only seeing his own shadow. We can tell that he is caught up in something that comes very much *from him* and is *about him*, and that it has very little to do with Annette. Freud called such experiences "re-editions" of past emotional situations. They are not precisely the same as childhood versions of the same pattern, but they are clearly in the same family.

It is characteristic of emotions that they are all too familiar. They convey no news, and are essentially re-editions of our past. Feeling, by contrast, actually brings us news from the outer world, connecting us to it in ways we never knew or had forgotten.

When Jack began to think about his earlier career, the emotional charge he had built up around his wife's supposed abandonment became transformed, through his relaxed focus, into a feeling about music. The sense of spaciousness that he conveyed is characteristic of feeling.

Emotions, after all, come in a limited range. We can name a few distinct emotions, perhaps up to a dozen or so, but not many more than that. There is no limit to the potential multiplicity of our thoughts — we can think about anything from Niagara Falls to the Pythagorean theorem to *Hamlet* — yet our emotions are suspiciously few. What have we got? Anger, fear, longing, satisfaction, joy, anticipation, jealousy ... They range from more pleasurable to less pleasurable, and they differ above all in the huge variety of thoughts that go with them. When was the last time you had a *new* emotion?

On the other hand, there is no limit to the feelings you can have, because there is no limit to the events and beings and things to which you can turn your feeling-attentiveness. *Feeling is emotion turned outward, received from the "outside."* As we begin to turn the rich, living, juicy quality of our emotional life away from our own sensitive souls, we can discover innumerable new feeling-experiences as that world impresses itself upon us. Every moment of experience could come to us with a new feeling-tone, if we met the moment with our full attention.

The kinds of inner experiences we all had as children far outstrip our normal adult experience both in range and intensity. When, as adults, we taste again the power of childhood feeling (often through a loss), it is always with a shock of distant recognition: "Oh, yes, the world can be this vibrant, this poignant." Then we wonder — and retreat.

As adults, we are less familiar with the experience of feelings that are either more intense than or just different from those of childhood and standard adult life. These completely new feelings can arise on their own in unusual situations. I remember the first time I became aware of this possibility. I was sitting with a group of friends when one of us confessed he had killed someone (while in military service). He was clearly agitated about this event, which had taken place many years before, and it was hard for him to bring the issue up to a group whose approval he craved. Someone asked him to elaborate, to tell us the details, and as he did I felt a wave of a completely new feeling. If I had to put it into one of the prelabeled boxes we put our emotions in, I might call it compassion — though I couldn't have said whether it was for him or his victim. But it was as distinct from my previous experiences of compassion as a whale is from a microwave. I can't now reevoke the feeling of that conversation; I only know how different it was, how strange and new. It was an uncharted experience of life, and it was specific to this particular story about killing.

Most of us can enter the realm of feeling through artistic experience. We know that for a composer, writer, dancer, or actor to be good at what they do, they must *feel* accurately and creatively, with a kind of sensitivity that is more than subjective. At the top of the manuscript for his difficult late Quartet in F Major, Op. 135, Beethoven wrote, "Must it be? Yes, it must be!" That is, he *felt* the rightness of what his mind at first rejected — and it was a rightness generations of grateful listeners have been able to confirm. It was not an emotion, but a *feeling* — not something about Ludwig or for the moment, but something about the music and outside of time.

When we appreciate the arts, as well as when we create them, we enter the same realm. They keep us from having an orientation that is exclusively intellectual, emotional, or utilitarian. They keep something fresh and available that the grind of daily practical life tends to kill. It is unfortunate that our experience of the arts today is tending more and more toward "entertainment" alone — toward experiences that simply whip up familiar emotions, rather than those that stimulate fresh understanding through feeling.

If we have this fantastic capacity to feel, why don't we explore it more? Why do we so obsessively practice the rush of familiar enthusiasms and the crash of familiar bitterness? What is it about us that keeps us trapped in the habitual display of anger, pride, jealousy, fear, triumph, and dejection?

Through emotion, we build a mistaken identity. A client comes in and complains about her stupid subordinate at work. From the sound of the story, it is clear the subordinate really is incompetent and foolish. But the problem for my client is how to let go of the self-righteous anger and disdain she enjoys at her subordinate's expense. For the more she emotes, the more secure she feels in how right she is, the more she enjoys the situation of her subordinate's stupidity and the further she is from working to find a solution to their difficulties. Our emotions always work like this. They build up the sense of self in a way that keeps it selfish, and we are seduced into enjoying them by telling ourselves, "It's the truth."

Social psychologists who study group behavior speak of the usefulness, for forming a group identity, of identifying an "out-group." A divided country can find a new cohesiveness once it is engaged in a popular war. A basketball team will feel they really belong together in the moments they are fighting off a threat from another team. A group of social activists will enjoy a sense of unity derived from fighting a certain industry or political group. These behaviors are not necessarily wrong, but they do tend toward perpetuating the situation of conflict: "outside" is inherently conflictual with "inside." My emotions do something similar: they affirm the sense of myself as situated over and against the world around me. Ultimately, they increase the sense that the world is unknowably *other*.

Feelings, by contrast, put me in dialogue with the world. As in a conversation, I both learn from the world and contribute something to it through my feeling immersion in it. I am not so radically separate from it — at moments, I may be completely identified with it.

To think a thought, any thought, we have to do it for a time. As you read this sentence: "Before the flowers of friendship faded, friendship faded" (Gertrude Stein), you have to think it through yourself to understand what it means. You cannot stand outside it completely and just observe it. *Afterwards*, of course, you can look at the thought and have your response, but in the moment of understanding the sentence, there is no distance between you and the thought. You are at one with it.

The identity of you with what you feel is, if anything, stronger. In real feeling, you meet the person, or thing, or idea, or being, with more of your whole self — more of your spiritual roots. You know it more thoroughly. In this process, there is always a risk. You are actually putting at risk more of who-you-have-been than in an act of thinking. We are far more willing to try on someone else's thinking (hard as that is) than to try on their feeling life. The slightest experience — watching a river flow, or hearing a breeze whisper through a bird's wing — if it is approached feelingly, can threaten all of who we have been. It would be almost as true to say that the river understands you as to say that you understand the river. Such an experience is unsettling.

This is why we so resist feeling: it threatens our security, our safety, our ingrained sense that we can stand pat with who we are, getting more and more, giving less and less. There is something in us that insists on being someone, on having a fixed identity, and this something doesn't want that identity toppled. The situation would be fine, I suppose, if only we had a high enough standard for selfhood. But we settle for an exclusively body-oriented identity at the cost of all other possibilities.

A friend who lived with the Kogi of coastal Colombia reports that as this archaic tribe tromped through the forest together, they would reach down into the ground when hungry and pull up a wild yam from under the leaves. After a few months with them, he said that he also developed the capacity to find yams this way. He said he didn't reason through where yams might be (nor could he). He just *felt* them. When a yam was needed, a yam appeared in his hand. This is close to the ultimate promise of learning to feel. It links us harmoniously with our surround. As Theodore Roethke put it in a poem, "the right thing happens to the happy man."

A wealthy and fierce businessman came to me because he had trouble sleeping. Since we are specially available to the spiritual world in sleep, I suspected that his problem had to do with the style by which he approached the world — an acquisitive style, unsuited to the world that sleep offers us as a gift. I suggested that he develop a certain kind of feeling just before bedtime. He could experiment with setting aside the computer, the newspaper, the television and telephone, and allow an hour or half an hour in the time just before bed to develop the feelings of devotion, awe, reverence, and wonder. I said he could do this by picturing some great artistic, political, or spiritual deed and marvel over it until the feeling grew stronger and stronger. Going into sleep this way, I assured him, would allow sleep to take him into itself more deeply.

As he listened, I could see that for a few moments he began to guess at the kind of thing I meant. For a few seconds, his whole body softened as he leaned forward, listening intently. Then his body stiffened and he put up one hand to stop me speaking any further.

"Hold it right there," he said. "Let's say I develop this sense of awe and wonder. *What's in it for me?*"

Even though I had said what was in it for him — that it would help him sleep — he could tell that there is something fundamentally at odds with egotism in the development of these feelings. They are not like other emotions. They open the self outward. Gratitude, awe, compassion, wonder, curiosity, surprise, reverence: these are the feelings that make us more receptive to whatever we meet. They put us at risk of changing our ideas and habits. They allow in the otherness, the newness of everyday life (as well as extraordinary life!), and so they make us more alive. They can destabilize us all the way into health.

The Practice of Feeling

There are two basic directions for practice with the life of feeling. On the one hand, we can dissolve, deconstruct, and transform emotions like anger. On the other hand, we can work directly with the creation of what I have been calling *feeling*. In practice, anything you do with one side of this equation also changes the other side. The goal of both kinds of exercise is fundamentally the same: We want to move from a world of separation to a world of connection, from an all-too-familiar world to a fresh world, and from a world in which we are mystified to a world that knows us deeply.

To dissolve our overemotionality, it is worthwhile first of all to see that we have some. You may think your every expression of irritation, your every annoyance, is simply how it has to be. In that case, there is nothing to practice. But if you suspect that your anger is at times excessive, that your worry and envy are a bit overblown, that your emotions are, in fact, suspiciously familiar — then you have a basis for playing with them and trying to see how they might be changed.

Let's say your anger is 90 percent unavoidable, justifiable, and written in stone. Ninety percent of it, the gods would agree, is perfectly right and good. Still, that leaves 10 percent to play with. So we'll just do our experiments with the 10 percent of the anger you are willing to transform.

Here is a way to begin. Think back to a time when you were angry. Call to mind the circumstances exactly. Picture the people or things that were around you and that seemed to cause your anger. Feel it again in your body. Rehearse to yourself, in your mind, the reasons for your anger. In other words, go ahead and recreate that same anger. Let yourself really experience the emotion all over again.

Now when you have succeeded in having yourself experience the emotion, let fall the "reasons." You evoked the anger by rehearsing them; now you just let them fall away. Instead of continuing to puff up the anger, you simply investigate it with an inner alertness. Find out what it is. You may notice that there are sensations in the body, such as tightness in the throat or belly. But these are not the anger, any more than the reasons are the anger. They are components of the total anger experience, but they are not anger itself. You are trying to find that third element, apart from bodily sensations and reason to be angry, which is the emotion itself.

This is a delicate inner work, as tricky as catching fish with your bare hands. As soon as you begin it, you may find the emotion disappears. You may find you do not know "where" to "look" inwardly. You may have to reevoke the anger by resorting to bodily tension and reasons again, just to have some anger to investigate. Yet if you persist and investigate, you will find something rare and strange.

The trapped emotion (anger or whatever you are using) will begin to shift and change. It goes through something like a transformation from solid to liquid. There are no names for this. We cannot say what the anger becomes; we can only say that it changes. You know it is the anger that is changing because you find (for moments at least) that the strength of feeling is undiminished, but that what you are feeling mutates, shapeshifts, and dissolves. It is no longer anger. It is a visitor from the new realm of feeling.

The released emotion becomes available for other tasks. It may turn out to be of the same substance as your life's best direction. This was the possibility expressed by Langston Hughes in his poem "Wave of Sorrow":

> Wave of sorrow,
> don't drown me now.
> I see the island,
> still ahead somehow.
>
> I see the island
> and its sands are fair.
> Wave of sorrow,
> take me there.[37]

Here the emotion is allowed, fully allowed, but the gaze is alert to a distant and noble goal. The experience is that the emotion actually helps to attain the goal — if we do not let it overwhelm us. In practice, this might be to take some spiritual and demanding text, in the very midst of your sorrow, anger, or other emotion, and immerse yourself in it. Or we can take the advice of John Keats ("then glut thy sorrow on the morning rose")[38] and bring our emotion-ridden minds to bear on some aspect of nature. We do not do any violence to the emotion, nor do we focus on it; we simply allow it to be present while turning the attention elsewhere. The higher the goal the better: a meditative phrase from the Bible or the *Upanishads*, an element of the natural world, a piece of music. Then we can discover that the very intensity of emotion, which we first held in a negative form, dramatically enhances our capacity to understand.

Immediately after rejection for a job for which I had applied, I happened to read a poem that had meant very little to me before, and it absolutely burst open with significance. It was a pure delight. Two weeks later, the job rejection long behind me, I reread the poem and found it again as flat as the first time I'd ever read it. The heightened emotion of the rejection had given me ears to hear with, for a time. Through the path of exercise, we attempt intentionally to build those organs of perception and keep them in play — even without bitter disappointment to help us.

Another, related way to dissolve fixed forms of emotion is to exaggerate them, not in retrospect, as in the first exercise, but at the moment when they arise in real-life situations. This is another of those techniques we can call "steering in the direction of the skid." Just as you gain control of a sliding car by first going with, then steering out of, the wrong direction it is taking, you can intensify a familiar emotion and so more thoroughly drop it.

We all know how to intensify an emotion. It isn't just something for method actors. All you have to do is think over the good reasons for it; picture the situation that causes it and its consequences; insist on it. The emotion will grow. If you are irritated that the elevator is so slow, you can make yourself angrier by thinking, "Those so-and-so's! They spend all this money on advertising and then they don't bother to keep up the building they lure you into! They can put a man on the moon but they can't make a decent elevator? The lousy people in there pushing buttons to the wrong floor and slowing it down. The dumb way people stand in the doorway and keep it open too long ..." (Don't display the exaggerated emotion outwardly, which would only waste the opportunity for practice.)

When the emotion has intensified a bit, you drop that train of emotion-justifying thought and turn to see what you've got left in you. In the first moment of mental silence that follows, investigate your inner life. This requires inventing for yourself the way to "look around" inwardly, not inside your body of course, but inside your heart and mind. If all goes well, you will discover that the original irritation begins to dissipate along with its exaggerated brother. You're left holding a kind of nothing: the original irritation, that had seemed so real, has become a capacity to feel. As in the previous exercise, this capacity can now be intentionally turned to an object worthy of feeling: a natural object, meditative sentence, or the possible encounter with a person near you.

The first of these exercises worked with imagining or remembering a moment of excessive emotionality. The second worked with intentionally exaggerating a real-life emotional situation. The third goes further into real-life experience. It involves simply renouncing all inward and outward exaggeration of emotion during a real-life encounter. If we observe ourselves closely, we find that our emotional responses are, so to speak, already exaggerated before we do anything with them. For example, we are absolutely appalled that our child has used the scissors to cut up a page in the phone book. Well, he has done just that on several previous occasions. It makes sense that we might be a bit annoyed, but our inner and outer tone of shocked outrage is an example of self-justifying emotionality that really can't be justified at all. The exercise works with this extra piece of emotion, the exaggerated piece.

We notice it, feel it, and drop it. The result is something like a return of a lost power — Native Americans referred to it as "calling back your spirit." The excess of inner life (what I have called the "extra") had lost itself into emotion; now it finds its way back to you. It becomes your capacity to attend again. It becomes love again.

All these have been exercises in transforming exaggerated or negative emotions. We now turn to a different kind of practice, which involves working directly in the realm of feeling to exercise a kind of perception we normally ignore or experience only around the edges of other functions in consciousness.

You might start with wonder. This is not a normal emotion, not directed to the isolated self, but a stance of the soul that opens us to the good. It is rarely portrayed in current popular culture, which tends always to reduce the world to known quantities. Real wonder can be invoked only through expansion, through an attitude that allows there could be something more than has already been known (and that this "something more" is good).

You need an object for wonder. It could be a person, but for adults the best objects are rocks, plants, or beasts, qualities (like honesty), capacities (like musical ability), or deeds (of generosity or self-sacrifice). For example, you might pick the power of approaching rainclouds in the sky and stimulate amazement at the phenomenon: that they float up there, that so much weight of water is somehow held suspended, the sense of grandeur or ease they convey, the wonder of the whole water cycle from cloud to river to sea and back again. What kind of universe is it that has such beauties?

In this kind of reflection, the aim is not to move into a scientific analysis of the phenomenon but to dwell in the phenomenon itself. Your thoughts are engaged in support of the feeling of wonder; they are not meant to define or limit the phenomenon in any way. Instead you may reflect that knowing the tonnage of water exactly would bring you no nearer to the phenomenon; nor would flying up among the clouds. They can speak to you just as you are.

It is possible, in such moments, for a new kind of feeling to come to light. It will tend to arrive when you are truly interested in the phenomenon, truly enthusiastic (from the Greek *en theo* = "in God"). It will surely not arrive at those moments when you wonder if you are doing it right. The mark of this new perception is that you *feel* the clouds, feel what they mean. You know they are "saying" in a language whose meanings are too huge to fit into human words. (We will return to sense perception as a meditation in the fifth chapter, "Opening.")

Another possible object for wonder could be any capacity in consciousness, such as thinking itself. You can proceed by asking deeply, and answering honestly, about the sources of the faculty you examine. You might wonder, for example, how is it given to us to start and then stop a train of thought? What gives us the (fallible) certainty that we have understood something? What gives us the (infallible) certainty that we have *not* understood something? Pondering and wondering, you might come to see that thinking, too, proceeds by feeling. You sense that our normal thoughts are accompanied by this feeling, which guides them with a sure hand. The sense of accompaniment, of being actively helped and guided in thinking, can grow very strong. It prompts a new question. *Who* is thinking?

When we practice the intensive invocation of wonder, reverence, or gratitude (see the last chapter, "Thanking"), we work in the realm of feeling. It is a form of understanding, and its practice leads to ever more and new understandings. As with every exercise, problems and distractions are relatively easy to describe, while the successful course of practice can only be loosely suggested. There are two sources of difficulty. On the one hand, each moment of practice is individual, and completely up to you to invent: repeating a model (such as those given here) will not help you. On the other hand, the experiences in question are unitive: they cannot be put into words, since words are tilted toward the world of duality.

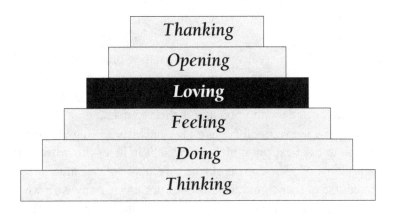

| Thanking |
| Opening |
| Loving |
| Feeling |
| Doing |
| Thinking |

The capacity to focus on what is good is no superficial graft from civilization, but a deeply rooted aspect of who we are. We often ignore this positive slant, yet our cynical or world-weary styles are the most superficial show compared with the fundamental optimism that keeps us talking and listening and reading. We can become more conscious of this largely unconscious loving, and draw it up ever more into evidence.

We trust the other car on the highway. We trust the other people in the elevator. We trust that it is worthwhile to say something — even if only to complain. We trust the cashier will give us the right change (at least most of the time). When we lose our grounding in this root attitude, in the optimism we almost never acknowledge, almost constantly deny — then we begin to be emotionally ill. When, instead, we intensify this most basic attitude, we find ourselves in love.

Love is first a confidence in the good, and then an attention to the good. As our positivity grows, we attend to the good more

completely, more creatively. The capacities practiced so far all
depend on this quality, which permeates every step of the Stairway. Thinking, doing, and feeling all show aspects of how love
operates. They depend upon it; it is their source.

To think is to speedily light on the next truth in a given topic,
to rush to the next point of meaning as if in love with what is to
be understood. The course of true love may not be smooth, but
the course of true thinking is. It does not linger lazily with what
has already been thought, but shoots forward, sometimes stum-
bles forward, like a lover rushing to be with the beloved. Thinking
that is worthy of the name does not hold itself separate from its
object, but immerses itself completely. Thinking then becomes, no
longer a thinking *about*, but a thinking *of* the very thing itself that
is thought. It loves the subject, merges with it, becomes one with
it, and even (in a sense) produces offspring with it. For this reason,
"knowing" in the Bible means sexual intercourse ("And Adam
knew Eve," Gen. 4:1). The most complete knowing is a total
entwinement, a generative contact: love.

Barbara Ann McClintock was to become a Nobel laureate in
biology, but as a young student in the 1930s she indulged in a
geology course and fell in love with rocks. Her biographer, Evelyn
Fox Keller,[39] tells that when the time came for the final exam in
this course, she filled one examination blue book after another
with her insights, throwing herself into the project with joy. As
she finished, she closed the last blue book and realized she had
neglected to write her name on the cover — and couldn't, for she
had forgotten her name. She had disappeared, if you like, into her
subject. She had become all rock. It was a quarter of an hour
before she had returned sufficiently to her location in a body and

biography to have her name return to her. This is thinking: it finds the good and forgets itself. It is love in the form of selfless application to its object.

When we do anything with our limbs in perfect attention, we go through a similar process. It turns us inside out, so that the sense of being "in here" (locked in the skin) and of the world being "out there" (apart from me) gives way at moments to a more expansive stance. We meet this often in the artists and athletes who feel they are not so much doing of themselves as participating in the world's own doing. Eugen Herrigel's Zen master, as he reports in *Zen and the Art of Archery*, used to say, "It is not I who must be given credit for this shot. 'It' shot and 'it' made the hit."[40] The quality of immersion is the central characteristic of what Mihalyi Cziksentmihalyi calls "flow," that is, of optimal human experience. The capacity of any activity to bring a practitioner to that experience is a big part of the love artists feel for their art, athletes for their sport, scholars for their discipline. Conversely, love of the activity is a big part of why it is conducive to flow.[41]

This flow is *doing,* and it brings us close to the sources of all movement. In any action intensively concentrated upon, the miracle of the fundamental capacity strikes us afresh. We see that the will *can* perform, that it *can* move our limbs, that it is both given to us and invites us beyond ourselves: all this is a form of love.

As a mature scientist, McClintock explained her uncannily accurate insight into the nature of the maize plant by saying that she had learned to develop a "feeling for the organism." As she sat in her Cold Spring Harbor laboratory, her attention would travel down the barrel of her ocular microscope and swim around, she said, in the cytoplasm of the cells she was examining. There she would "feel" what processes were going on, and experiments later confirmed her in her radical discoveries.

This is feeling: through an intensification of the process of thinking, a further immersion and attentiveness, we feel our way to new truths about the object under investigation. It demonstrates a nonutilitarian, nonmanipulative love for the world that invites the world's response.

One of Steiner's favorite examples for such love is the Persian legend about a master walking with his disciples. They come to the putrid, rotting carcass of a dog in the road. The disciples turn away in disgust. The master however approaches the carcass and looks at it calmly, then remarks, "What magnificent teeth."

The love or positivity here is not blind. The master of course recognizes the presence of all the ugliness the disciples emphasize. Yet his attention moves quickly to find the good. The point is not to pretend that what is ugly is beautiful, but to appreciate the beauty that is present.

Well-practiced, the capacities on the Stairway all involve two intimately entwined but conceptually distinct kinds of selflessness: renunciation and receptivity. On the one hand, they require instantaneous renunciation of what has been attained. The expression "you can't take it with you" finds its ultimate relevance here. In this case, it's not about possessions that can't be retained after physical death, but rather it's about not trying to possess the fruits of the last instant of time as it dies into the next. You find that you can't keep the last insight, the last good moment of achievement, the last perceptive feeling. You can't take it with you into the next nanosecond. Our normal sense of self is composed precisely of keeping: we look in the mirror and see who we have already been, creatures of the past. To love is to abandon this incessant greed and live in a constant process of giving away every treasure. It cuts deeper than many apparently grand gestures of renunciation and kindness (which may be undertaken for egotistical aims) but is their true basis when they are authentic. This kind of love lives in the microgesture, within consciousness itself.

On the other hand, such loving requires a selflessness on the receptive side: making place in one's soul for the other to appear *as* other. Rainer Maria Rilke has a poem called "The Seer"[42] in which he emphasizes how we must fight to be taken over by the new, but especially by the sacred. "What we struggle with — how small it is! What struggles with us — how vast!" He has the insight that when Jacob wrestled with the angel, his achievement lay in *losing*. To be vanquished by a divinity is to win beyond one's previous reckoning. Speaking of the seer, Rilke writes that "victories do not interest him. He grows by being deeply conquered by what is greater — and greater still."

This aspect of loving is the most threatening and the most unbelievable, even impossible, and yet it happens all the time. It is the basis of each day's unconscious learning. For every time we say of someone, "she has grown," "he is wiser now," "they have learned a few things," we are saying that they have somehow allowed themselves, willy-nilly, to be conquered by a greater truth than they previously embodied. In the vicinity of all learning, we can notice the footprint of this selfless love.

Steiner said that in the storms and confusions of the soul, thinking was the beacon that offered a point of surety. Freud felt the same way, though he called it consciousness rather than think-ing. Both were aware of the saving grace of awareness itself. How-ever much we find our minds inadequate, or doubt their capacity at times, we have a fundamental and abiding trust in our capacity to understand that only leaves us in moments of real insanity. As I said at the start, we always trust our *current* thinking, even if we doubt previous thinking. If we declare thinking useless, we unwit-tingly declare its perfect functionality, for we are trusting our cur-rent thought that thinking is useless.

Such confidence, unshakeable even when it goes unacknowl-edged, is not confidence in a thing but in a capacity. Therefore, strictly speaking, it is confidence in nothing. For what supports us so unshakably is not this or that understanding, but that we *can* understand. And it is just the same with feeling and doing. We are not supported by their results, but by their reach — the very fact that they are there. And this fact is given to us: no one does any-thing to deserve it. We awake into self-awareness and find our-selves able, astonishingly able, to think, to feel, and to do. People are fond of quoting Aristotle, who said that philosophy begins with wonder, but they often assume it is easy to wonder. Yet we typically lose the trick of wonder and awe after our earliest years, and by the time we have the self-awareness to even notice the functions of consciousness — thinking, feeling, moving, dream-ing, perception, mental pictures, memory — we have grown too insensitive to be in awe of them.

Our ground or point of stability is thus invisible, intangible, soundless, and odorless — though richer, livelier, and even (you could say) "earthier" than all of these. *Love* is not sentimental "love," but involves a deep, willingness. While we have already (and undeservedly) been given this willingness by life itself, it remains up to us to actualize it or not.

As the examples from McClintock's life show, what we talk about when we talk about love is, from another standpoint, attention. We say of children that they "want attention" — meaning they want our love. And we notice that when we love a book we can attend to it, stay in it, dwell in it, while if we do not love the book we will tend to avert our gaze and attention from it. When we are "in love," the beloved is everything to us, and we don't notice anyone else. We are fascinated, involved. When we are not particularly in love, our eyes wander from our current partner to some other conversation, and we wish we were there.

Normally, we are conscious only of this or of that, not of the attention itself that attends to this or to that. And if we try to turn our attention *on* attention, we have the problem that, once again, what we have in view is at best some past act of attending, or the kinds of things we attend to, but not the current act of attention itself. As we noted in the chapter on thinking, we arrive on the scene of awareness a moment too late.[43] We miss our current attending (of which our current thinking is a special case), and find instead something in consciousness that has already been attended to. We are as if condemned to the past.

Its own sources are invisible to normal consciousness. They are what Kühlewind has called "superconscious" — brighter than normal awareness, and outside it.[44] As we begin to intensify our concentration, this realm of the roots or sources comes ever more into view. The possibility does exist of seeking and finding the attention itself, which is actually outside of time but appears as if "before" it becomes this or that to which we attend. *In the attention, as the attention*, there is nothing to describe, because attention itself is not *like* anything known; it is not one of attention's objects. No graven images!

On the one hand, this brings us in the neighborhood of the statement that God is love. To put it in the terms we have used so far, *the source of the world is (superconscious) attention*. On the other hand, seen from the psychological side, it brings us to an understanding of what it might mean to say that we are made "in the image and likeness of God" — since we are given the possibility to know and be this attention through every act of concentration. John Scotus Eriugena, the great ninth-century Irish Christian mystic, said that the soul in prayer (that is, at its peak of attentiveness) becomes indistinguishable from God in the same way that iron in the forge becomes indistinguishable from the fire.[45] In every tradition, there has been an awareness that the intensification of human consciousness through prayer or meditation brings it into unity with the sources of being.

Rilke asks, "When *are* we?"[46] It might seem that we always are, so that this is a silly question. But Rilke means to suggest that there are times when the sense of the real intensifies, and we become freshly aware, with wondering awe, that we exist. And he more or less answers his own question by saying that it is not through longing or through effort, not through what is normally called love, but through "being breathed by God" — an effortless immersion. He points up the difference between *this* loving and all ordinary kinds. As we need to be vanquished by ever-greater adversaries to arise to our true strength, we can only find our true being, the awe of it, through immersive and effortless attention.

Loving is not in the zone of effort, but in the life that comes after much effort — effortlessly. It isn't hard. The angels are not depicted as sweating out their next moment of praise, but they give their gifts in joy. If we, since Adam's curse, must get our spiritual nourishment "by the sweat of our brow," yet when the nourishment finally arrives we find we have somehow already left off work. At such moments it is the Sabbath, no matter the day of the week.

At its most approachable, loving means that we seek out what is good and put our consciousness there. When I consult with companies about management issues, I ask employees to compare how often they complain about co-workers with how often they praise them. The overwhelming emphasis is on blame. I ask how much time they spend during the day concentrated on their work and how much time they spend concentrated on the problem level — the manager who oversteps his authority, the employee accused of stealing. If they search their hearts before answering, they acknowledge that at least as much time is spent (fruitlessly) on the problem level as on the substance of their work. Why?

Well, it is easier to blame than to praise. If I am really praising, there is nothing in it for me. It's about you. Like all concentration, whether on work or play, concentration on the good is selfless. To put it another way, blame, like emotion, gives us an easy (though illusory) self to be, and we do have that profound, unstoppable, undeniable urge to be. We settle for the easier path, always the easier path.

There is a place for criticism, of course. We don't have to be mindlessly accepting of everything that we meet. But the healthy place for criticism is right in the midst of love. It is not the criticism that sets up the critic as better and above what is criticized, but the sharp clarity of the gardener who shears away what is dead or overgrown.

Through concentration we approach the source of awareness. We awaken to an existence not bound by the body and its brain. This kind of being comes only through an infinitely extended focus on what is good. It comes through loving.

The Practice of Loving

The anecdote about the master and the rotting dog with magnificent teeth can serve as our initial guideline. We want to shift the balance of our awareness, even if only a little bit, in the direction of magnificence. We want in this way to offset the inherent gravity of life on Earth, with all Earth's troubles. We want to lighten up. We want to tip the scales in favor of the good.

A first practice is to think about the people closest to you. La Rochefoucauld, the seventeenth-century French wit, once said, "Christ enjoins us to love our enemies, but that is child's play. The great thing is to love your friends." And indeed it is easy enough to "love" and "forgive" and even "pray for" the terrible people we read about in the newspapers or hear about on TV. But can we forgive our nearest and dearest for the little things they do that really annoy us?

Picture a situation in your life that has apparently negative elements in it. Reflect on it; see the players involved; replay it in your mind. Really sense the difficulty, the intractability, of the situation. Then seek for the good that is already present in it. The point, once again, is not to deny what is ill, false, or ugly. The point is only to see if you can focus on elements in the situation that are positive. They must be truly seen, not made up from nothing. Allow the focus on these good elements to grow so intense that your sense of the situation changes from one of resignation or despair to one of hopefulness. You will automatically find that you adopt a more inventive inward stance: you discover ways the positive elements in the situation might grow.

I witnessed a wonderful application of this principle at Harlem Hospital. The staff all wanted Kyanna, a ten-year-old girl with advanced AIDS, to join a support group for children who knew about their diagnosis. Her mother was a former prostitute and current alcoholic who, in her deep shame, refused to tell Kyanna about her AIDS and wouldn't let any of us tell her either, which meant she would not be able to join the group. This reluctance and shame were all too likely: after all, Kyanna's AIDS had been transmitted to her at birth. After many fruitless attempts to convince the mother that Kyanna needed to join this group, and so needed to be told her diagnosis, we decided to try one more time. Suddenly Kyanna's pediatrician, Elaine Abrams, grew silent for a moment. She looked at the mother in a new way. She saw her, not as a difficult alcoholic who was impeding her patient's well-being, but as a good woman struggling with an unbearable load. The resistance to telling Kyanna her diagnosis changed from being an

ultimately selfish avoidance to a completely understandable version of her love for Kyanna. Elaine put her hand on the mother's
knee and said, "Julia, what are you doing for yourself to get
through all this?" It was not said manipulatively, yet it had a mirac-
ulous effect. After crying for a time, Julia agreed that Kyanna
should know about her illness and should go ahead and join the
group. The cold surface of resistance had melted through the
warmth of Elaine's loving.

The second exercise in *loving* will take you from addressing
problem situations in fantasy to addressing them in daily life. It
involves predicting in advance that a certain interpersonal situation will be difficult, and then, when it arrives, focusing on the
possibilities, what Kabbalists call the "good seeds," that lie dor-
mant within it. Again, such elements must be perceived, not
invented from whole cloth. See if the situation can *feel* different,
more promising, less *about you*, before you try to say or do something to improve it. Then say or do something to improve it.

As with most exercises, the practice includes a great deal of *not*
doing. Much is achieved by restraint, by simply refraining from
normal negative judgments and reactive patterns. In the pause that
follows an inward act of restraint — a pause that may take no
clock time at all — there is the possibility of invention and generosity. My teacher, Richard Fulmer, Ph.D., used to say that in
treating couples he always looks for "the generous offer." This is
the moment when a husband or wife will argue for a split second
on the other person's side, make an offer or suggest a perspective
that is outside the role of antagonist. Such moments, he pointed
out, are easy to miss, and they can disappear if no one notices and

promotes them. To allow the generous offer to grow and be accepted, both the therapist and the couple must refrain from their assumptions of how the "enemies" will behave.

Over time, the effects of this exercise will gradually or suddenly astonish. Your reactivity changes. You become less insultable. You change from a sufferer to an inventor of the day. The people around you, without losing a single flaw, grow more precious. You become available to subtle presences and processes previously overlooked, ignored, or forgotten. The day becomes more alive around you. Instead of escaping from life into some abstraction of goodness, you find that the morning is made of virtue, and time itself bends close to whisper its secrets in your ear.

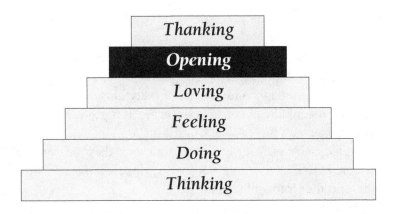

We live in a finished world. There are no openings. The oak tree never tries to become a peach, let alone to become a giraffe, and the quartz stays quartz. There's no invention or fantasy or originality in nature; no possibility of surprise, for instance, in the planets and asteroids. With enough data, NASA could predict them all. It is a finished world.

There are unforeseen circumstances, of course. The weather is notoriously hard to predict. Elk may stray further south than they've ever been seen. Extinction happens. But all this plays out the way it had to play out. Even those songbirds whose songs continually vary learn only slightly new songs with each generation. At least in principle, the world of nature is fixed.

It is the same with us. How often do your friends surprise you? Our children and our spouses, and we ourselves, react in most situations with a deadening predictability. We read the newspaper and learn that everyone the world over is doing just what they tend to do. The students in the classroom, the pundits in the paper, nearly always make the same kind of point. And while the world's hot spots vary a bit, human aggression and self-interest, the destruction of the planet, seem constant.

Somehow, though, and in spite of everything, we can't quite shake off the inkling of potential freshness. It is just barely possible that we could surprise the world. Humans are, ultimately, the least predictable element in all creation, since they are potential creators as well as creatures. Somewhere under all that ash, there still lurks the gleam of living fire.

New creating depends on new seeing. So our first task in opening is to overcome the closedness in our perception, the fixed and finished quality of the world we imagine around us. For us to surprise the world, in other words, the world has to surprise us.

We were starting to drive to a friend's house, and my son Rody, then five, announced, "We're going to school!"

"No," I said, "the beginning of our trip today is *toward* school, but we're going further, to Steve's house. We're not going to school."

"Oh, yes we are!" insisted Rody. "This is the way to school. We're going to school."

It went back and forth like this a few times. Finally I just said, "Let's see."

The moment came when we didn't take the last turn to school, but drove on past. Rody looked around in delighted astonishment.

"I was *wrong!*" he shouted, utterly gleeful.

Now that's a talent we lose in adulthood: the ability to find genuine pleasure in being wrong. Our inability in this regard is just one symptom of the sickness we call a normal sense of self. Freud referred to the ego as "the dominant mass of ideas," and it is a telling phrase. For it is the mass of ideas that tends to be dominant, not we ourselves. Our apparently triumphant, confident everyday self is actually the product of being dominated, unwittingly, by all that we take for the truth. We are "happy" insisting that we are right, not delighted to have been wrong.

A more playful and spacious sense of self comes when, like small children, we can see our position upset and be tickled with its demise. Try *that* in an argument, though. Just try to take the other person's view and be delighted with it, renouncing your own. You will feel your own stuckness — the sticky, ungiving quality of excessive attachment — and you may also catch a whiff of the secret shame we all bear from a lifetime of insisting on our rightness.

It is necessary for opening to come after loving. For if we developed a kind of radical openness before strengthening our fundamental orientation to the good, we would put ourselves in harm's way. With a greater vulnerability, we would be susceptible to even more of the horrors of our world and would take their dismal tendency for the only truth. After all, there is always more than enough evil and stupidity in the world to justify despair. By schooling ourselves first in love's positive slant on the universe, we are likelier, as we open our hearts even in the face of disaster, to invent an adequate response and not to dissolve in depression.

In psychotherapy, I am continually impressed with my patients' ability at times to step outside their accustomed "take" on the world and, in flashes of wholeness, come up with new possibilities. One young woman, attractive and accomplished, found herself always flirting and then sleeping with the boss at her various jobs. She spoke about these affairs with an air of inevitability, as if they just had to happen. I listened. Another affair would occur; she would feel miserable with herself; she'd lose the job eventually; then the cycle would start again at the next job. Of course she tried to seduce her therapist too. I just listened. Sometimes I asked about her past. She'd had a sexually provocative uncle who may or may not have done something transgressive to her when she was in kindergarten. This vein of memory seemed promising, but nothing in therapy helped her to withstand the next temptation at the next job. Meanwhile she had a boyfriend she was always on the point of leaving. He sounded like a rat.

And then one day she had a change of heart. She came in and announced that she was quitting her current job and marrying that rat of a boyfriend. From one day to the next (though it took three years in therapy to arrive at this point) she stopped the pattern — and it stayed stopped. She said she looked at her boyfriend in bed that morning and saw a completely different person. It was not the familiar experience of seeing one's spouse and feeling as if he were a stranger. Instead, she looked at someone with whom she'd continually argued and saw him as deeply lovable. Her boss, by contrast, she perceived in all his shallow opportunism.

She came back for a visit years later, so I had the chance to follow up: a happy marriage to the "rat," beautiful children, no new affairs, and a change of career that made more use of her creative talents.

Only among humans does one find such radical change. It depends on this capacity for opening beyond our current prejudices. One of its most incredible forms is forgiveness, that rare instance of beginning. In the documentary *Long Night's Journey into Day*, which is about South Africa's Truth and Reconciliation Committee, you can see remarkable examples. Through the work of the committee, murderers face the surviving relatives of those they have killed. There is often a tremendous release of rage at these encounters. Sometimes, however, mothers will forgive the murderer of their own children. It certainly does not come from denying their grief and rage. In one episode, a black man who worked for the (white, Afrikaaner) police force confesses to a group of black women whose sons he had helped to kill. They heap abuse on him as on a murderer and traitor. He acknowledges his crimes and begs forgiveness. Slowly, through many tears and recriminations, they make a turn, and embrace him. The friends I saw the film with all felt the shock and the reproach of this episode: could we ever forgive our children's murderer?

We all know that being closed off from the world is not a complete error, but a matter of exaggeration. It is not that boundaries and habits, knowing and familiarity, predictability and stability, are so terrible. We rely on constancy in ourselves and others just as we rely on the ground not to suddenly shift like quicksand under our feet. A measure of stability in our outer and inner worlds is necessary, like the tail on the kite that anchors its flight. It is truly wonderful that the tree in the garden is still there after so many years; it is glorious that two and two still make four; it is a blessing that you kept your promise. The problem is not with the world's constancy or with our own steadfastness, but with our neglect of the inventive spark, the unprejudiced regard, that we also need so desperately. Too much openness, and we would evaporate. Too little, and we ossify. We become the unforgiving victims of our own habits.

For most of us, the problem is ossification. Steiner referred to it as "prejudice," a state of being trapped by one's own judgments.

And he emphasized that freedom from such prejudice is an essential aspect of the process of self-development, of learning to give our gift to the world. When we begin to look closely, we notice that we are excessively closed off or prejudiced both in familiar "macro" ways and in the tiniest "micro" aspects of consciousness.

As a clue to the nature of our "macro" prejudices, consider this story from a colleague of mine at Harlem Hospital in New York City, when I worked in the Pediatric AIDS program there. Nancy was African-American, like the rest of her family, but she did have a cousin who married a white man. Nancy and her two daughters would often see this man at family functions — weddings, reunions, holidays — and her girls knew and loved their Uncle Sid. At a family cookout on the beach, when the girls were seven and nine years old, they were chatting with him when one of them looked at him suddenly and said, "Uncle Sid! You're *white*!"

They had simply never noticed before. They knew their uncle for his humor, his personal style — for what he *meant*. They knew him in his uniqueness, not in his generality, and so they weren't involved in assigning him to a fixed category like black or white. Our "macro" prejudices derive from those moments when we begin to judge situations or people by outward characteristics and disregard the specific meanings they express. Even though it was developmentally appropriate for the girls to be able to see that Sid is white, it would be unfortunate if they could now *only* see him as white.

"Micro" prejudices operate in the same way, but they are more pervasive and more subtle. As a result, they tend to escape our notice — so much so that it is hard to give examples of how they work and what it might mean to be free of them. They actually pervade all the functions of consciousness, giving us a relatively deadened world. We have considered some of how this works in thinking, to some extent: the tendency to dwell in thinking's past products rather than in its processes. And we have looked at the way our emotions grind on like machinery, predictably insisting on "me, me, me."

By contrast, we have barely touched so far on the question of everyday sensory perception, though this is the preeminent form of "micro" prejudice that permeates our waking life and is rarely refreshed. Normally we assume that the world just is the way it appears to the everyday consciousness of our time, or we overlay on our own perceptions a supposedly scientific fantasy notion that the world around us is "really" a bland collection of molecules and forces. These have none of the intensity, the feeling charge, of the world drenched by memory and meaning: the smell of pine needles that reminds us of a lost love; the intake of breath as we face a magnificent cloudscape. It seldom occurs to us to take as real those moments when the world appears *more* qualitatively rich and poignant. Encouraged by a scientizing worldview, we think of such moments as emotional enhancements of a cold, sober reality. But we are in good company indeed when we begin to imagine that our moments of excited perception may be the truest.

The poet William Blake summed up this view by saying that "if the doors of perception were cleansed, we would see everything as it is, infinite."[47] Poets and mystics, like archaic peoples, have always claimed that our very senses — sight, hearing, smell, and so on — can deliver us to a world of sacred meaning rather than a world of meaningless things. And just this is what the world's demanding traditions have referred to by seeing the origin of the universe in the Word — proclaimed, for example, in both the Jewish and Christian Bibles.

You can approach this stance intentionally by a kind of thought experiment. Call to mind a special place on earth, a place that means a lot to you, a place that can fill you with longing or melancholy or excitement. Most people have returned to some spot, if not as adults then as children, and found that the place itself was resonant with significance for them. To a newcomer the place would not look like much, or it might look attractive but without that enrichment of past experience. It wouldn't mean much to them. Now imagine a style of looking that was as enriched, as brimming with significance, the first time something was seen. The meanings the landscape held for such a style of looking would not be based on past experience; they would be meanings inherent in the landscape itself. Imagine that such meanings were experienced as so intense that the visual stimulus paled by comparison — just as, when we read a book, we can become so involved in the story that we barely notice the page we are reading it from.

This more intense seeing, which dwells in what the landscape is revealing rather than in any past association or current visual image, would be a seeing freed from our normal prejudices. Rilke describes such a moment of seeing in his essay called "Experience." He tells of leaning against a tree, in a state of perfect relaxation, and becoming gradually aware that a kind of oscillation or wave emanated from the tree and permeated him, filling him with the peace, the embeddedness, that is at the heart of the tree. He never makes the mistake of suggesting that the meanings of nature are like our normal meanings, or like anything in the realm of human speech. He is open to the news from nature.

In another way, a text for this more open seeing is the great first section of Psalm 19, in which King David praises, by harp and by song, the created world:

> The heavens recount the glory of God
> and the firmament tells the work of His hands.
> Day to day utters speech,
> and night to night speaks knowledge.[48]

What is so striking here is the Word-like quality of all that is. "Recounting," "telling," "uttering," and "speaking": this is what the world is up to — and they are all forms of expression.

What David seems to be saying is that when we cleanse the doors of perception, we not only have before us an infinite and sacred world, but more exactly an expressive world, a world that reveals meaning. From this position, we ourselves become capable of making new meaning. And we only arrive at such a position when we can begin to look without imposition of our accustomed categories. We would need to overcome, for example, the prejudice of thinking that the senses deliver us a world "out there," while we are "in here" — inside our skins. We would need to overcome the prejudice that what meets us in sight is essentially a visual phenomenon. We would have to overcome, for moments, the conceptual categories by which we already know what *that* is: a tree root, a snowfall, a seashell, a birdcall. Leaving all past knowing behind, we can unweave these "micro" prejudices — so ingrained and automatic we scarcely know how to locate, let alone release them — and meet the world in one unobstructed clarity.

After a good conversation with a friend, it can happen that you don't know who made what point or to whom an idea first occurred. You have dissolved the narrow identification both with your physical body and with the body of your private emotions. In the same way, good seeing brings us into dialogue with the land-scape, the tree, the stone, the animal, and at moments we are no more separate from this world than we are from our own current thoughts.

The Practice of Opening

In the privacy of your own mind, in the secret moments of your own heart, why not admit your "macro" prejudices to your-self? What group do you mistrust, as a group? Do you have inner reservations against whites? Blacks? Gays? Women? Men? Chil-dren? Management? Labor? Muslims? Jews?

These may not be the categories that are relevant to you. See if you can find the ones that *are* relevant. But in addition to groups, think about those people you "already know" about — friends, family members, or colleagues whose conversation is dull or oth-erwise unwelcome to you. Go ahead and make a list, for your eyes only, of these "macro" prejudices, which (however you may justify them) keep you always a bit separate, a bit closed off.

Now imagine one person you know, or one person from the group, and see this person, in imagination, as potentially open to new ways of seeing and being. Picture the person as an infant, then as an old man or woman; picture the person hurt by injustice; picture the person at a moment of surprising good fortune; picture the person at the moment of death. See if, through this picturing, you can allow a more spacious attitude toward the person. Be careful not to use these imaginings as an occasion to confirm your prejudice; allow yourself to experiment with a positively tinged mental picture. Allow yourself to see the person you distrust as capable of the good and especially of the new. Note down your experience.

If you have the opportunity, a next step here is to seek out such a person, or several, and see if you can bring some of the openness of your imagination into lived experience with them. Can you share a joke with them and enjoy their response? Can you learn something valuable from them? Can you see them as suffering? Can you encourage their success and appreciate their struggle? Note down your experiences afterward.

You will find that the very willingness to open to them changes your whole inner stance. Instead of getting the predictable (though ever-diminishing) pleasure of seeing your prejudices confirmed, you will taste a very different kind of pleasure, which has nothing to do with your likes and dislikes. It is the pleasure of potential and of unpredictability. Don't start with the most difficult person or group; start with your less self-righteous prejudices and work your way up.

As a second stage, we can supplement this "macro" practice with the undoing of a "micro" prejudice — that is, one of the kinds of prejudice that informs our everyday waking consciousness all the time. You can work with sense perception, for example in the act of seeing.

In the first chapter we discussed how every act of sight is governed by the concepts we bring to it. Other cultures and ages see a different world from the world of our normal adult perception, since they do not see with our concepts.[49] Something similar can be observed among adults who, born blind, have been operated on so that their eyes perform normally. Numerous studies have shown that they do not see the world we see, because their sight is devoid of the usual concepts.[50] It is, relatively speaking, unprejudiced.

Practices in the direction of meditative perception do not return us to the seeing of children, of archaic peoples, or of those born blind who are given sight as adults. The very process of arriving at a new kind of seeing by our own effort makes what we might attain completely different from these cases, which are all unwilled. Our orientation and preparation are also different. Still, we do regain some aspects of these other kinds of perception, while encountering altogether different qualities as well. For one thing, we are prepared consciously to allow that the world is itself *expressive* — that it radiates sacred meanings toward us continually, meanings to which we are normally unreceptive. "Day to day utters speech." Therefore the work of meditative perception is first to undo our normal sight, to let go the concepts that permeate our everyday seeing, and to open ourselves to what might be coming toward us from the physical world.

We are likelier to do so if we have already developed a capacity for intelligent feeling — the feeling that *knows*. Thinking can then release words and concepts because there is a sense for something more, and more essential, behind them.

Steiner said that we don't perceive all we could in the physical world because of the "counterkick" of our own ideas.[51] That is, we are continually projecting our habitual concepts onto the world about us. The world is beaming its high meanings in our direction, and we kick against them with the whole conceptual structure derived from our language, culture, and upbringing. Dissolving this structure for moments will not make us impractical dreamers or turn us into imbeciles, capable only of dumb wonder. Our familiar conceptual structure snaps back into place all too quickly. But for moments, for brief periods of practice, we can allow a little more dumb wonder into our lives. We will not suffer by it.

Take a hard, natural object, like a stone, a twig, or a shell. It is good to work with hard objects, because they last over many days of practice. It is good to work with natural objects, because the goal is to deepen perception in the direction of nature's own ideas, and man-made objects (composed, of course, of natural elements) only distract us with the human ideas stamped into them. It should not be a particularly beautiful object, and certainly not one with sentimental associations.

Set your object on a table or chair arm beside you and look at it in detail for thirty seconds or so. Notice its surface, its texture, the marks on it, and its overall shape. You will see that there are no *words* for most of what you perceive of its details — subtle differences in color or contour. Yet there are *concepts*: *this* bit looks just *this* way. You have a conceptual lock on every aspect of what you are seeing.

Now close your eyes for a moment to reorient yourself. Your next look will be very different. You will open your eyes briefly and just take in the stone as a whole — all of it at once, with its details, but no longer enumerating them to yourself one after the other. Open your eyes and do this whole seeing for about ten seconds.

Alternate these two very different kinds of looks two more times: details of the stone, then the stone as a whole; and again, first details, then whole. See if you can really make these two looks distinct from one another and appreciate their distinctness. In both cases, you are doing something we normally never do by lingering with a single perception and intensifying it. In both cases, you are cleansing perception from the normal prejudices and distractions that plague everyday seeing. Yet in the "details" look you are continuing the process of conceptual overlay that is at the basis of normal perception, while in the "whole" look you are relaxing this overlay a bit and beginning to allow the stone itself to approach you.

Let's take this one step further. Again we alternate two ways of looking at the stone. In this case, though, the first look will be the shorter one — just five to ten seconds — and the second will be longer — thirty seconds or more. For the first look, we are going to exaggerate just what is problematic in everyday seeing; for the second, we will swing completely over to the other direction.

The first look goes very much from you to the stone. You already know what the stone is. It is merely a stone. It is over there, while you are over here. There's nothing to learn from it. At most, you might briefly think you could use it for something — like a doorstop, or an object to throw at someone. All this exaggerates our normal dismissal of the world, its relegation to a dead physicality.

The second look is as if from the stone to you. You have the inner attitude of allowing, of welcoming whatever the stone might want to reveal to you. You impose nothing. You gaze with "soft" eyes. Your inner speech might be "Please reveal yourself." You put yourself in a state of visual wonder. Whatever the stone already looks like, or has already revealed, you are willing to set aside as you welcome its continuing radiance.

Again, pursue these two looks through two more repetitions: you to the stone, stone to you; you to the stone, stone to you. Really feel the difference, the extreme difference, between these two kinds of seeing. In one, there is nothing to learn from the stone; in the second, there is no end to what you might learn from it.

The stone can begin to shift both in terms of how it looks and what it means. It can begin to flow and to become suggestive. It can grow precious to you, dear as a beloved human being. It can seem to expand or contract, to grow transparent. It can become central in the way normally we are central to ourselves while the world about us seems peripheral. At a workshop of mine, one participant reported that the stone — a nondescript piece of gravel — had become "almost unbearably sensual." All are changes in the direction of greater significance. This can increase immeasurably. The stone, which was previously a thing, is revealed as something like a word: before, we only saw it as a jumble of letters (sense perception); now we read its meaning. At the end of the exercise, close your eyes for just a moment and then open them softly to gaze at the ordinary objects nearby. The first moments of perceiving after a perception exercise or after a meditation can show you a washed world (Paul Célan's phrase).

This exercise, quite apart from its implications for our understanding of the physical world, can help soften and release the
whole realm of prejudice, both "micro" and "macro." The stone,
the twig, the shell can reveal themselves uniquely, but so can the
human being we have previously boxed into a category. The first
exercises in this section, involving relationships with people, are
strengthened in new ways by meditative perception. The two lev-
els complement and reinforce one another.

Another exercise benefits just from this interaction. Toward the
end of the day, you review the day (in writing, or vocally with a
friend) so as to answer the following three questions: What sur-
prised me today? What moved me today? What inspired me
today? The mood of openness that this exercise creates can both
illuminate the day behind and prepare you well for the realm we
call sleep.

Through such practices of opening, we begin to approach
events, as well as things and beings, with a greater flexibility. We
become less swift to judgment and anger, more receptive to high
influences and inspirations. What was previously closed begins to
open. Events lose their hard surface and become transparent,
responsive, spacious. We need less protection from life. Predictability gives way to unpredictability. We don't know what will
happen next. We will receive it. We will create it.

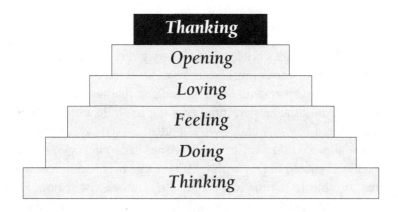

| Thanking |
| Opening |
| Loving |
| Feeling |
| Doing |
| Thinking |

We started *thinking*, and we end *thanking*. Whether or not there is an etymological relationship between the two words, there is a substantive link between the two acts. We can be grateful to the extent that we appreciate what is given to us — to the extent we can think it. And we can think all the better if our thoughts are supported by gratitude. So the first step supports the last, and the last returns us to the first. It is not a stairway with a top step, but a rhythmically ascending spiral with no upper limit.

The practice of the Stairway always involves turning away from the past toward the present moment and the future. Where normal thinking, for example, is content with its own past and notices only its own past products, we have been interested in the present instant of thinking's self-blossoming. Where normal perception is content with the already known world that stands in opposition to its viewer, we have been interested in opening to a current world that expresses itself to us afresh. The sixth step on the Stairway, thanking, works the same way. We aim at thanking, at gratefulness, not only for gifts already given, but for what just now is coming into being, and for what is yet to come.

When we are grateful for something, at that moment it has a freshness as of the new creation, even if it has been around a long time. When our first child was a toddler, a friend came over to play and picked up a toy truck that Asher had long neglected. As the friend started to play with it, Asher came over and found that that dull old toy of his had acquired a renewed fascination. He didn't want his friend to play with it and grabbed it away. What struck me so forcibly was not this moment of jealousy, but that for a few days afterward Asher continued to delight in the toy as if it had been made new. The touch of his friend's attention had worked like a magic wand waved over the truck. It brought an old toy into the zone of freshness. Maybe anyone can say, "Behold, I make all things new." Whatever we are grateful for is new at the moment of our thankfulness, and whatever we pay attention to becomes new.

If you want to increase the presence of gratefulness in your life, it is certainly worthwhile, as many of our grandparents told us, to count your blessings. There are innumerable objects, events, and people for which we can be grateful. Yet this is not something anyone *has* to do. On the contrary: thanking, like the other steps on the stairway of surprise, is a completely free activity. We sometimes insist that our children say "thank you," but we cannot insist on thankfulness itself. Normally it either wells up or not. We have all been in the position of saying "thank you" and not meaning it, and perhaps of giving a gift and hearing a "thank you" that rang false. Real thanks doesn't have to be given for reasons of social form, or for any other reason. In fact it doesn't have to obey the rules of reason. Nor does the real giver insist on thanks, but only receives gratitude, if it comes, as a second gift. When thanks truly are given and received under the sign of freedom, we can often dispense with words. All it takes is a glance.

In 1980, I was lying atop the roof of a novitiate house in a Muslim slum in Calcutta. I had come there to volunteer with Mother Teresa's Missionaries of Charity in their work with the poorest of the poor at Kalighat, her home for dying destitutes. All day we scooped up the sick and dying from the filthy streets of Calcutta, brought them to Kalighat, bathed and fed and clothed them. Then we watched them die. I noticed that the dying men we tended were grateful and ungrateful for our attentions in ways neither I nor the Indian Brothers quite understood. They might be indifferent to the meal that (temporarily) saved their lives, then tearfully grateful for being propped up on a rolled-up towel. The extreme conditions of disease and starvation made them sensitive to the slightest touch or gesture.

It was the end of my first week, and I was sick with dysentery. All about me, on their bedrolls, the male novices slept after their day of feeding and tending to the poor, the leprous, the insane. I was awake, between trips to the bathroom, in excruciating abdominal pain. Far above, on that unusually clear night, stretched the Milky Way with its countless stars. As I lay there, hearing only the occasional sounds of street fights below, I reflected on the poverty and disease I had seen all over Calcutta. My own pain — though about as much as I could take at moments — was trivial compared with the fantastic extent of suffering throughout Calcutta. I thought of all the prayers of thanks that the missionaries sang and prayed, and, directing my thoughts up to the stars, I silently asked how anyone could be thankful when the world was so full of misery. Then a strange thought occurred to me: that no one could really say they had ever thanked God — or had been thankful at all — unless they had been thankful for suffering too.

Something happened then. While still lying on my bedroll, I was also up there, among the stars, or else somehow they had come down to me. It was an extraordinary sense of freedom. And the stars bore a message. It was not in the words, not even in the thoughts, of my normal mind. At this remove of time, I can retrieve only a glimmer of what was meant, but this glimmer seems like a current utterance, still speaking after all the intervening years. On the one hand, it made clear that yes, one can thank for suffering, at times. Beyond this, though, it set suffering in a wider context — the context of being. We can thank for existence itself.

In this chapter we will look at several kinds of thanking, but they all are set in the wider context of gratitude for the very fact of being. The particular kinds of thanking finally tend to serve this one, and if the other practices we have discussed have any depth, they will tend to deliver us into the arms of an endless gratitude for being itself: that we exist, that the world exists, and that in this world are other beings.

If someone were to ask, "What *is* it to thank?" or "What does the word 'gratitude' mean at all?" we may find ourselves stumped for an answer. "Oh," we might say, "it's a feeling you get, a feeling of ... of, well, *thanks*!" Thanking at first seems like one of the basics of human life, as fundamental as breathing, love, or hate. Still, we can look at it a little more closely, find ways to enhance it, and so allow it to become the next step on our Stairway.

To be thankful for anything, we must first perceive it. Infants cannot be said to be grateful in the first moments of life. We have to mature into a perception of the world as given before we can see it as a gift. It must be known as something out there, next to us, in front of us, for us to be grateful for any part of it. So gratitude, in a sense, is only possible after the Fall. We first need a world separate from us, and then we may have some response to it, whether of resentment or of gratitude. It has been said that infants do not need to pray because they are still at one with the sources of being — they do not need to *relink* themselves through *religion* (whose Latin root, *religere*, means just that: "to relink").

In this fallen world, separate from us and noticeable by us, we are precisely not grateful for most of it. We give thanks only for something that distinguishes itself from the general mass of things and events — something specially noticeable and different. It is a good difference, or we wouldn't be thankful (at least until we can give thanks for suffering and being itself). Finding ourselves in the presence of the good, we are relinked to the good through this quality or feeling or stance we call "gratitude," "thankfulness." The Hebrew word *kadosh*, or "holy," originally meant "set apart" — distinguished for sacrifice or worship.

Thankfulness typically moves from one person to another, creating or developing a kind of intimacy. I can be grateful for a gift without knowing who gave it — more wonderingly grateful, since I don't reduce the unknown giver to known categories. Still, someone gave it. We don't really thank inanimate processes: the moment we thank water for flowing it becomes animate, a person. Or else, by thanking, we are putting ourselves in relationship to a being who composed water in the first place. And thanking makes us more present as persons too. We come into being, we begin ourselves anew, when we thank. Ultimately, in every act of thanks we link ourselves to the Creator who, on making all the world, found it good.

This goodness of the created world is the good of speech, the good of expression. This has been the view of most of the world's religions. In ancient Hebrew, for example, there was no word for "thing" at all — and perhaps there were no mere things for them in their resonant, significant world. The term used in modern Hebrew for "thing" is *davar* — one of the ancient terms for "word." This choice expresses the understanding that every thing, properly seen, is a word.

Whenever we are grateful, we are involved in something wordlike, in a meaning, and so we approach an understanding of the world as created by the Word. The gift means something to us. It speaks. It says, "You thought of me," "You love me"; or the gift means, "Now I can do this," or "The world is this good." Or just, "Here's this." Beauty itself carries a meaning not to be put into words: it means exactly *that* — that particular beauty. In many languages, the word for "world" is related to the word for "light" — for example, the Romanian *lumen*, which means both "light" and "world." Whatever we find in this world that partakes of the light, whatever signifies, can be a source of thanks.

To thank is to concentrate, to focus on the particular gift at hand, even if the particularity in question is the whole universe. Of all that is, I focus somewhere, and my thanks is for that object of my attention. Any focus, any act of concentration, will move us in the direction of gratitude to the degree we have already practiced thinking, doing, feeling, loving, and opening. Thanks comes not only through a direct practice of thanking, but through the harmonious working of all the other practices that heighten our attention. So all our meditative practices, involving as they do the concentrative power of the heart and mind, heighten our capacity for thanks.

Attention itself has an aroma of goodness about it. Some social psychology studies have shown that overly strict authority is better for children's development than total neglect. Mere attending to something makes it seem good to us, which is the secret of our misplaced veneration for celebrities and "personalities" of all kinds, including spiritual leaders at times. We redeem this quality inherent in attentiveness when, instead of being manipulated by our culture, we choose our own focus of attention and seek the good in it. Then we find that gratitude is also there.

A friend from Switzerland signed a note to me, "I wish you good work and wonderful meetings." She didn't mean business meetings. She meant encounters with other people. Her words reminded me that, from my parents onward, I have been blessed or cursed with innumerable encounters that changed what was possible for me and opened me to new vistas, or else closed them off. What meetings have changed your life? Have any of the encounters been fruitful? Have you been grateful enough for the good ones to actually take the lessons they taught? Have you been someone good for others to meet? By signing her letter with that salutation, my friend made me aware of a whole field of potential gratitude that I had largely ignored. It made me realize, too, that I tend to think only of past meetings, while she was wishing me wonderful meetings in the future. Perhaps we have not met all the people who will be truly important to us. Just as there was a time before we met our mates, a time before we had our children, this moment is a time before the next meeting that may also be a great addition. Can we be grateful in advance for the very possibility of new friends?

So much depends on whom you have met, and the most important people in your life may not be the powerful ones, the ones who could "help" you in any outer way, but the ones with whom something emerged that was uniquely present during the encounter and that fostered your life in ways you can sense but not measure. Of many such encounters, I could mention one that came during a period of intensive meditative practice two years ago.

Having dropped my car at the mechanic one day, I needed a ride, and a very old man who had just picked up his own car offered to give me a lift to the train station. We chatted on the way there. I asked him about his Veterans of Foreign Wars bumper sticker and about his Vegan bumper sticker, since they seemed an unlikely combination. The conversation was all about him, since I was curious about his life. After about a five-minute ride to the station, I got out of the car and said, "Thank you so much for the lift." Instead of just saying, "You're welcome," the old man fixed me with a penetrating yet mild glance and said, "Don't worry about anything. Ever. Because it won't help."

I burst out laughing, and he drove away. What a gift! As I walked to the train and found a seat, I felt as if a load of worry I didn't even know I was carrying had been lifted from my shoulders. All that day, I was practically skipping. It was a meeting that has stayed with me, though I don't know the man's name and will probably never see him again. He knew just how to give his gift, and I still benefit by it. May we all have such meetings in our future.

Another category of event for which we often neglect to thank is the category of obstacles. One of my teachers, Paul Wachtel, startled me by writing in the acknowledgments section of his book that he wanted to thank his wife and children for getting in the way of his work. He realized what a blessing it was to have them there as impediments! It meant that he had a life, a far more important focus than his book, which was constantly taking him away from his writing. As a writing husband and father, I now know what he meant.

We could take this inkling further and give thanks for all the obstacles that keep us from our goals. For one thing, they make us heft and sense the true value of the goals in a way the smooth and easy course could never do. They offer a contrastive balance too; we can sometimes realize that a goal is not worth our while given such obstacles. If we do persist in our aims, we must find the inner resources to overcome or cooperate with our obstacles, perhaps to incorporate them.

One of my grade-school teachers told me there could be no story without conflict, and I was intent on proving him wrong. So I wrote a story about a garden that I tried to drain of all tension, all conflict. It was achingly dull. I ended up agreeing that conflict is necessary for a story, and so it is with the story of our lives as a whole. No obstacle, no life. A deeper immersion in this theme can give us a dawning sense of what is called fate or karma. Like our meetings, our obstacles whisper to us of a larger life in which this life is unfolding. Obstacles present us with our horizons, and give us the chance to extend them. Is it impossible to give thanks, today, for the obstacles we have yet to face?

We do not know how we do any of the things we do. We don't know how we think, speak, or move. We don't know how the mysteries of feeling and love come to us. It is all a gift. We are the recipients of the most tremendous blessings even when we think that nothing much is happening. These are the fundamental, ineradicable goods of consciousness itself. No logician can give a reason for why this or that argument seems evident. Ultimately, behind any supposed rules of logic, we must rely on a sense of evidence that is just a feeling — a bright feeling for truth — but whose source and style are initially unfathomable. By focusing on the functions of consciousness, sensing their preciousness, and feeling our way toward the source of their mysterious availability, we can bring ourselves to the very edges of everyday consciousness. At times, our grateful wonder can make these edges dissolve as we sense our way right into the region of the sources. Then we have a new horizon of wonder.

The exercises in this book have aimed at purifying the fundamental processes of the soul, that is, of attention in all its forms: thinking, feeling, doing, and so forth. When we add this element of thankfulness to each of them, we find out still more about them. Gratitude acts as a further invitation to the attention, helping it to reveal itself to us, coming ever more into the light of awareness. At blessed moments, we know that we *are* the attention that is coming to light.

Inner aspects of thinking and feeling do not necessarily express themselves in familiar ways, such as through words or images or any other element of pastness, but they do disclose themselves to us. In the presence of gratitude, they become at once more conscious and more inward. Gratitude can be quick, but it does take a moment of doing, and in this moment the timelessness of our attention can make itself felt.

In Steiner's formulation of the six exercises, he set forgiving in the sixth place. By harmoniously rotating the previous five, he said, a mood of reconciliation or forgiveness would arise in the soul. I practiced it that way for many years, and I am sure Steiner is right. We all bear a fantastic grudge against the world, and the exercises each work to undo this basic resentment. They allow us to forgive, which requires of us a new beginning, or at least to transform our resentment so that it becomes like that of Robert Frost, who wrote for his own epitaph: "He had a lover's quarrel with the world."

A Buddhist teacher once told me that as long as you are insultable you are not enlightened. With each progressive enlightenment, we become a bit less sensitive to slights. We can forgive them. Through forgiveness, more of the energy of the soul can go into the intensive cultivation of its talents — what Rilke called our "glad powers" — and less into nursing our wounds.

Through the practices themselves, I have found that forgiveness leads to thanking, and so I have given thanking as the sixth practice. To really forgive is not just a neutral state of letting bygones be bygones, or of putting the old offense out of mind. It is to turn around and actually thank the offensive person or situation for what has occurred. As I said before, no one can make you do this, and you do not have to do it. Still, it is possible.

Those who have suffered real horrors — rape, solitary confinement, concentration camps — sometimes report that, along with elements that they cannot forgive and elements that seem purely evil, there were gifts embedded in their situation for which they can be enduringly grateful. It is customary for psychologists to downplay such insight as "rationalization," as if theoretically to undo the achievement involved. I am more willing to take people at their word.

When trekking in Nepal, I met an Italian mountaineer who had once nearly drowned when his ship sank. He and ten others had been in a lifeboat for forty-five days in the Pacific before they were found. He told me about throwing the dead overboard, about the real terror of exposure to the sea in its fury. He said that at one point they had so little with them that the ration for a whole day was to lick the top joint of your index finger, stick it in the sugar bag, and suck the sugar that adhered. He lost fifty pounds. As we talked over his adventure, he told me it had permanently harmed him in the sense that he still had nightmares about it years later, and he still sometimes found himself weeping over the anguish he felt and the lives that had been lost. At moments he still could taste a bitter rage against those who had let the ship go down, destroying so many lives. But his time in the lifeboat had also given him enduring gifts, and he was grateful for them. For one thing, it became a measuring stick. If he could master *that*, he was often thinking, he could master *this* — whatever problem life threw at him. As a result, he said, he had become much more active and professionally successful since the shipwreck. He said he was no longer afraid of death. "Out there," he had touched on moments of complete reconciliation to death, which he could now retrieve at will. So he gave thanks for the depth and breadth of what the experience gave him, although, or rather because, it was a disaster.

Forgiveness is the beginning of thanks, and then thanks has no end. It is possible to imagine a contemplative order whose whole profession would be thanking and nothing else. They would be doing the rest of us an enormous service. Instead of the airwaves and thought waves that perpetuate the world's resentment, such an order would send out a quality that helps to marry heaven and earth ever more intimately. Thanks reaches into the sources of the world, and brings creator and creature close together.

The Practice of Thanking

A preliminary practice to developing gratefulness is to find and ponder a question that is a real one for you. It won't do to ask a question with no edge to it, for example, to ask someone else's question. A real question for you might be about some meeting that has changed your life. Or it might be about something apparently less personal, like an economist's question about the routes of distribution of grain. It might be a philosophical question, such as the nature of time.

As you begin to put the question to yourself, perhaps not for the first time, try to approach it from the ground up, as if it were the first time. If your thinking plows deeply, you will come to moments of unknowing, of openness, the brink of a promising nothingness. The question, which can be about something quite practical, begins to open you.

As you turn the question over in your mind, you can shift inwardly to include thanking. You can marvel at the very fact of the arena that has come into view, the specific zone of unknowing the question presents to you. You ask, for instance, "What kind of world is this where time is possible at all? Where does time come from? Who made it? *How* can I think it?" Because of your earlier work in loving, the accent of such questions is positive, and the blessing of the question comes ever more to the fore, even if the question goes unanswered. You become like a meadow grateful for rain. The rain is that you can *ask*.

This practice brings us the possibility for gratitude even if we don't get what we "want" in some area of life. It is essentially an exercise in intentionally bringing wonder, the attitude of marveling, into play through addressing a question that is important to us. Through such wonder, we can find ourselves grateful in directions, depths, and dimensions we previously ignored.

Another exercise in thanking is to stimulate a sense of thanks at the moment your feet touch the floor when you rise from bed in the morning. The very repetitiveness of the action comes to serve as a reminder: this is the moment to be grateful. Yet your gratefulness is a creative act each morning, and not repetitive at all. It is up to you somehow to stimulate gratitude at that moment.

You might be thankful for a specific blessing that occurs to you, or for the whole of being. As you practice this regularly, you will find that it becomes possible to stimulate the actual experience, the feeling of thanks, with very little substance to be grateful for. It is like a fire that somehow needs less and less straw in order to burn with the same brilliance, until finally it can burn with no straw at all. You wake, swing your feet over the bed to the floor, and along with the miracle of waking an intense gratitude is there.

Steiner used to point to the benefits of rotating the five previous exercises, practicing one a month, and we have already considered that they jointly contribute to the practice of thanking. Here is a further application of the same idea, but in miniature. In less than five minutes you can tell over the previous five exercises, one by one, and bring to mind the living quality of each of them in turn. I call it "rotation."

For example, you call *thinking* to mind: that it is possible to focus on a given area and deepen your sense of it, ever less encumbered by distractions; that thinking always takes place in the present; that its roots are invisible to ordinary awareness; that understanding is always invisible; that we are not separate from our thoughts, but *in* them. You then shift and bring *doing* to mind: the miracle of our being able to move the body at will; the benefits you have felt from doing a simple action with entire focus. You bring *feeling* to mind: how you can refrain from exaggerated emotion, yet deeply feel the truths in all that surrounds you. You bring *loving* to mind: that the attention can leap toward what is best, find the gem in the mud, and endlessly merge into its object without losing itself. You bring *opening* to mind: the ability to drop memory and expectation and know the world as a conversation rather than as a collection of objects. These phrases are just examples and are useless to repeat. They are suggestions for how you might ponder the Stairway as a whole and briefly evoke a living sense of each distinct step.

This exercise of rotating mentally through the five earlier practices can end with a moment's gratitude. You give thanks that the soul can be extended in these directions through practice, that practice is possible at all. The soul's perfectibility is itself a gift, perhaps the greatest possible gift, including as it does our freedom *not* to perfect the soul, but to leave well enough (or ill enough) alone.

It is helpful to practice this kind of rotation before any other meditative theme or prayer you undertake. It prepares you for immersion in the theme you are about to focus on. By briefly immersing yourself in each of the six qualities, you find that you can bring more of yourself to the meditative theme that will follow. It is a way of gathering your powers towards the single point of the theme. You will be less likely to dissipate your attention in associations and distractions. A five-minute rotation of the six exercises is also beneficial before an important personal encounter, or at the beginning of the day.

Thanking, like thinking, is manna that cannot be stored. It lives in the moment of its own performance, or else it putrifies. Thanking that has become lazy turns into the anxiety that you will lose what you have. This is no longer thanks: it is an aspect of insecurity, if not of greed. Thanking does not grab onto the gift, but simply delights in it. We can think of a gift — even if the gift is something intangible, like time itself — as wanting a hug from us but not wanting to be chained by our affection. Thanking leaves the gift free.

If we intensify our gratefulness sufficiently, it grows dense, like the other soul functions, and becomes a self-sufficient activity. We no longer need anyone to thank, or anything to be thankful for. We become thanking itself, a part of the gratitude at the heart of creation, and it is more than enough.

NOTES

Throughout this book, details about psychotherapy patients have been changed to maintain confidentiality.

Introduction

1. Plato, *Phaedo*, in *Great Dialogues of Plato*, trans. W.H.D. Rouse (New York: New American Library, 1956), p. 485.

2. Steiner's six "supplementary" exercises, always given slightly differently, can be found in a number of places in his works, for example, in *Guidance in Esoteric Training* (London: Rudolf Steiner Press, 1994), pp. 13ff.

3. David A. Cooper, *God Is a Verb: Kabbalah and the Practice of Mystical Judaism* (New York: Riverhead, 1997).

4. Ralph Waldo Emerson, "Merlin," in *The Early Poems of Ralph Waldo Emerson* (New York: T.Y. Crowell, 1899), p. 159.

5. Robert Frost, "Birches," in *Robert Frost: Poetry and Prose*, ed. E.C. Lathem and L. Thompson (New York: Henry Holt, 1972), p. 54.

6. Rudolf Steiner, *The Essential Steiner*, ed. Robert McDermott (New York: Harper & Row, 1984).

7. Ibid.

8. Georg Kühlewind, *From Normal to Healthy*, 1988; *The Life of the Soul*, *Stages of Consciousness*, 1984; *The Logos Structure of the World*, 1986; *Becoming Aware of the Logos*, 1985 (all published by Lindisfarne Books, Great Barrington, Mass.); also *Working with*

Anthroposophy (Great Barrington, Mass.: Anthroposophic Press, 1992).

9. Ralph Waldo Emerson, *Essays and Lectures*, ed. Joel Porte (New York: Library of America, 1983).

10. All biblical quotations, unless otherwise noted, are from the King James Version.

11. Buddha, *The Dhammapada: The Sayings of the Buddha*, trans. T. Byrom (New York: Vintage Books, 1976), p. 3.

12. Emerson, "Experience," in *Essays and Lectures*, p. 475.

13. Emerson, "The Oversoul," in *Essays and Lectures*, p. 385.

14. Dogen, *Moon in a Dewdrop,* ed. K. Tanahashi (San Francisco: North Point, 1985), p. 70.

15. Emerson, "Experience," p. 472.

1. Thinking

16. Henri Ellenberger, *The Discovery of the Unconscious: The History and Evolution of Dynamic Psychiatry* (New York: Basic Books, 1970). See also L.L. Whyte, *The Unconscious before Freud* (New York: Basic Books, 1960).

17. Sigmund Freud, *On Creativity and the Unconscious* (New York: Harper and Row, 1958).

18. J.L. Benson, *Greek Color Theory and the Four Elements: A Cosmological Interpretation* (Amherst, MA: University of Massachusetts Libraries, 2000; library@umass.edu/color.jpg).

19. Noam Chomsky, *Aspects of a Theory of Syntax* (Cambridge, MA: MIT Press, 1965). Most linguists today, including Chomsky,

would assign the ultimate source of the child's linguistic attunement to the brain.

20. Blaise Pascal, *Pensées* (Paris: Garnier Flammarion, 1973), p. 128.

21. Emerson, "The Oversoul," in *Essays and Lectures,* p. 385.

22. Emerson, *Journals,* entry of May 13, 1835, quoted in burtslaw.com homepage.

23. Bodhidharma, *The Zen Sermons of Bodhidharma,* trans. Red Pine, (Berkeley, CA: North Point Press, 1987), p. 31.

24. William Shakespeare, *Hamlet,* act 3, scene 3.

25. Ibid.

26. W.B. Yeats, "The Circus Animals' Desertion," in *The Collected Poems of W.B. Yeats* (New York: Macmillan, 1951), p. 335.

27. Emerson, "The Oversoul," p. 385.

28. Simone Weil, "Reflections on the Right Use of School Studies with a View to the Love of God," in *The Simone Weil Reader,* ed. George Panichas (New York: David McKay, 1977), p. 45.

29. Otto Palmer, *Rudolf Steiner über sein Buch, die Philosophie der Freiheit* (Stuttgart: Verlag Freies Geistesleben, 1966), p. 71.

30. *Katha Upanishad,* in *The Upanishads,* trans. J. Mascaro, (New York: Penguin, 1965), p. 65.

2. Doing

31. John R. Searle, *Expression and Meaning: Studies in the Theory of Speech Acts* (New York: Cambridge University Press, 1979).

32. Cf. the discussion of the limits of a brain theory of consciousness in K. Popper and C. Eccles, *The Self and Its Brain: An Argument for Interactionism* (London: Routledge and Kegan Paul, 1977), and Jane Healey, *Endangered Minds: Why Children Don't Think and What We Can Do About It* (New York: Touchstone, 1990).

33. Rudolf Steiner, *The Study of Man*, trans. Daphne Harwood, Helen Fox, and A.C. Harwood (London: Rudolf Steiner Press, 1966).

3. Feeling

34. Bodhidharma, p. 47: "To leave the three realms [desire, form, and formlessness, comprising all existence] means to go from greed, anger, and delusion back to morality, meditation, and wisdom."

35. Kühlewind, *From Normal to Healthy*.

36. Daniel Goleman, *Emotional Intelligence* (New York: Bantam, 1995).

37. Langston Hughes, "The Island," in Hughes, *Selected Poems* (New York: Knopf, 1954).

38. John Keats, "Ode on Melancholy," in *The Norton Anthology of Poetry* (New York: W.W. Norton, 1975).

4. Loving

39. Evelyn Fox Keller, *A Feeling for the Organism: The Life and Work of Barbara McClintock* (New York: W.H. Freeman, 1983).

40. Eugen Herrigel, *Zen and the Art of Archery* (New York: Pantheon, 1953), p. 85.

41. Mihalyi Cziksentmihalyi, *Flow: The Psychology of Optimal Human Experience* (New York: Harper and Row, 1990).

42. Rainer Rilke, "The Seer" (*Der Schauende*), in *Rainer Maria Rilke: Werke in Drei Bänden*; Band I (Frankfurt: Insel Verlag, 1966). My translation.

43. Cf. Friedrich Hölderlin, "But friend, we come too late!" in *Alcaic Poems* (New York: Ungar, 1962).

44. Kühlewind, *The Logos-Structure of the World.*

45. Duns Scotus Eriugena, from "Patrologia Latina" in *The Age of Belief: The Medieval Philosopher,* ed. A. Freemantl (New York: George Braziller, 1957).

46. R.M. Rilke, *Sonnets to Orpheus,* I:3.

5. Opening

47. William Blake, "The Little Black Boy," in *The Norton Anthology of Poetry.*

48. S.R. Hirsch, *The Psalms: Translation and Commentary* (New York: Feldheim, 1997), Psalm 19, p. 135.

49. Alan Ereira, *The Heart of the World* (London: Cape, 1990).

50. Marius von Senden, *Space and Sight* (Glencoe, IL: Free Press, 1960).

51. Rudolf Steiner, GA 198, lecture of July 10, 1920.

6. Thanking

52. Arthur Deikman, *The Observing Self: Mysticism and Psychotherapy* (Boston: Beacon, 1982).